4

wrong side. Cut a piece of paper-backed fusible web the same size as box band. Fuse web to wrong side of box band; fuse box band to box. Fuse web to wrong side of fabric for lid. Use pinking shears to cut a circle slightly smaller than top of lid and a strip slightly narrower than rim of lid; fuse to box. Add "stitches" around box using a black fine-point permanent pen. Glue torn fabric bows and/or buttons to box band.

- **Banner** — Paint design (pgs. 130 and 131) on a 14" x 20" purchased canvas banner. For border, fuse paper-backed fusible web to fabrics. Cut 1"w strips of fabric of varying lengths. Fuse border pieces to edges of banner. Glue buttons and jute bow to banner. Insert dowel in banner; glue knobs to dowel. Tie jute to dowel for hanger. Glue jute bows to dowel.

PAGE 4

- **I've Been Good Sweatshirt** — Paint design (pg. 36) on shirt.
- **Baby's First Christmas Romper** — Paint design (pg. 36) on romper. Fuse paper-backed fusible web to wrong side of fabric. Cut hearts from fabric; fuse to romper.
- **Towel**— Paint design (pg. 122) on muslin. Fuse paper-backed fusible web to wrong side of painted design. Use pinking shears to cut painted design into a 2½"w strip the width of the towel; fuse to towel. Use embroidery floss to add Running Stitch (pg. 166) along edges of strip.
- **Star Basket** — Paint design (pg. 122) on muslin. Fuse paper-backed fusible web to wrong side of painted design; fuse to poster board. Cut out painted design. Add "stitches" using a black fine-point permanent pen. Glue painted design to basket. Tie raffia bow to handle.
- **Vest** — Paint design (pg. 27) on vest. Glue buttons to vest.
- **Merry Christmas Sweatshirt** — Paint design (pg. 124) on shirt. Sew torn fabric bows and buttons to shirt.
- **Greeting Card**s — For each card, color design (pg. 30 or 64) on card stock. Spray with glossy wood tone spray. Use decorative scissors to cut out design. If desired, glue colored paper to back of design using spray adhesive and cut around design, leaving a border. Fuse paper-backed fusible web to wrong side of fabrics. Cut fabric to fit front of purchased card and envelope flap, using pinking shears if desired. Fuse fabric to card and envelope. Cut heart or star from fabric; fuse to envelope. Glue design to front of card using spray adhesive. Decorate card with raffia or jute bows and buttons.

BACK COVER

- **Let Heaven and Nature Sing Wreath** — Paint design (pg. 144) on fabric. Cut a piece of cardboard slightly larger than painted design area. Cut painted design 1" larger on all sides than cardboard. Center cardboard piece on wrong side of painted design. Fold fabric over edges of cardboard; glue in place. Glue jute around edges of painted design. Glue painted design, jute, naturals, and torn 3"w fabric strip bows to an 18" dia. artificial evergreen wreath.

- **Tree Skirt** — Paint design (pgs. 67 and 68) on a purchased canvas tree skirt. Fuse paper-backed fusible web to wrong side of fabric. Use pinking shears to cut ³⁄₄"w strips of fabric. Fuse fabric strips around tree skirt. Glue torn fabric bow and buttons to tree skirt.
- **Stocking**— Paint design (pg. 29) on a purchased canvas stocking. Add "stitches" around edge of stocking using a black fine-point permanent pen. Fuse paper-backed fusible web to wrong side of fabric. For cuff, cut a fabric strip to fit top of stocking; fuse to stocking. Glue buttons to stocking.
- **Chambray Shirt** — Paint designs (pg. 109) on shirt. Fuse paper-backed fusible web to wrong side of fabrics. Cut fabric rectangles to fit between the buttonholes. Cut a piece of fabric to fit on shirt pocket or flap. Fuse fabrics to shirt. Machine appliqué (pg. 166) fabrics using clear nylon thread. Sew torn fabric strip bow and buttons to shirt.
- **Gift Tags** — For each tag, color design (pg. 114) on card stock. Spray with glossy wood tone spray. Use decorative scissors to cut out design. Glue colored paper to back of design using spray adhesive; use decorative scissors to cut around design, leaving a border. Punch hole in corner of tag.

GENERAL INSTRUCTIONS
TRANSFERRING TO LIGHT-COLORED FABRIC OR CARD STOCK

Before transferring a design, use a small test transfer included in the book to determine the best iron temperature and length of time needed for a good transfer.

1. If you are transferring a design to a fabric item that will be laundered, first wash and dry it without using fabric softener.
2. Preheat iron for five minutes on appropriate setting for item being used. Do **not** use steam.
3. If transferring to fabric, place a clean piece of fabric or paper under the fabric so that transfer ink will not bleed through.
4. Place transfer, **inked side down**, on **right side** of item. Place iron on transfer; hold for five seconds. Do not slide iron. Pick up iron and move to another position on transfer so areas under steam holes are transferred. Carefully lift one corner of transfer to see if design has been transferred. If not, place iron on transfer a few more seconds.

TRANSFERRING TO DARK-COLORED FABRIC

Trace design onto tracing paper. Place tracing paper, **traced side down**, on right side of item; tape or pin in place. Insert a light-colored transfer paper (such as Saral®), **coated side down**, under tracing paper. Use a stylus or a dull pencil to draw over lines of design.

PAINTING YOUR PROJECT

1. If the item you are painting will be laundered, use either fabric paints or a mixture of half textile medium and half acrylic paint. If the item will not be laundered, use acrylic paints.

Continued on pg. 166.

7

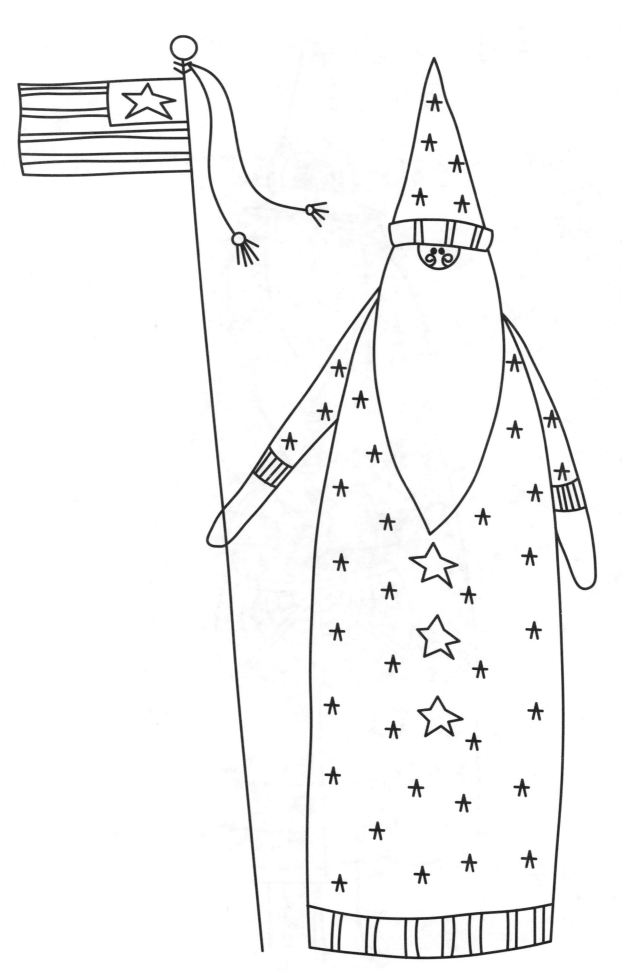

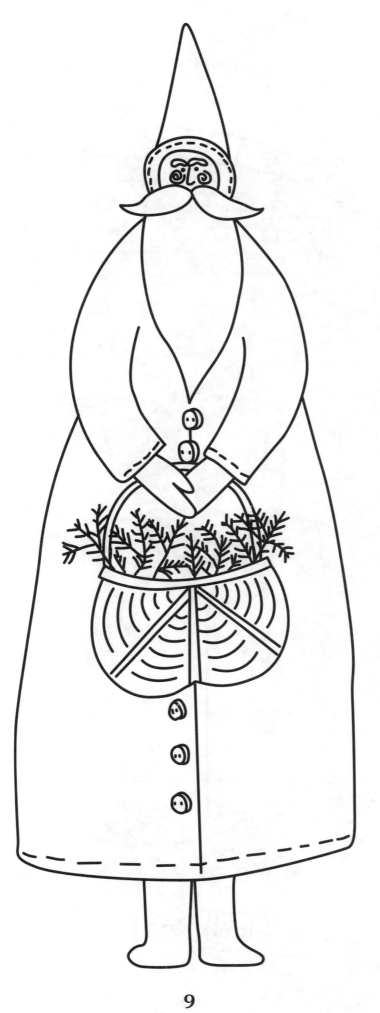

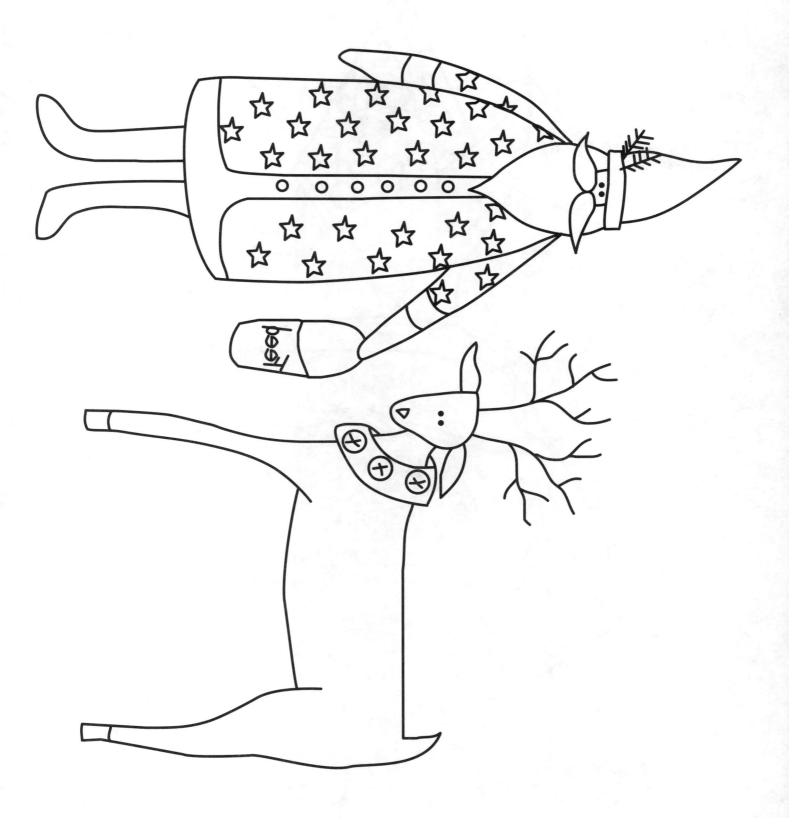

11

Merry Christmas

 />

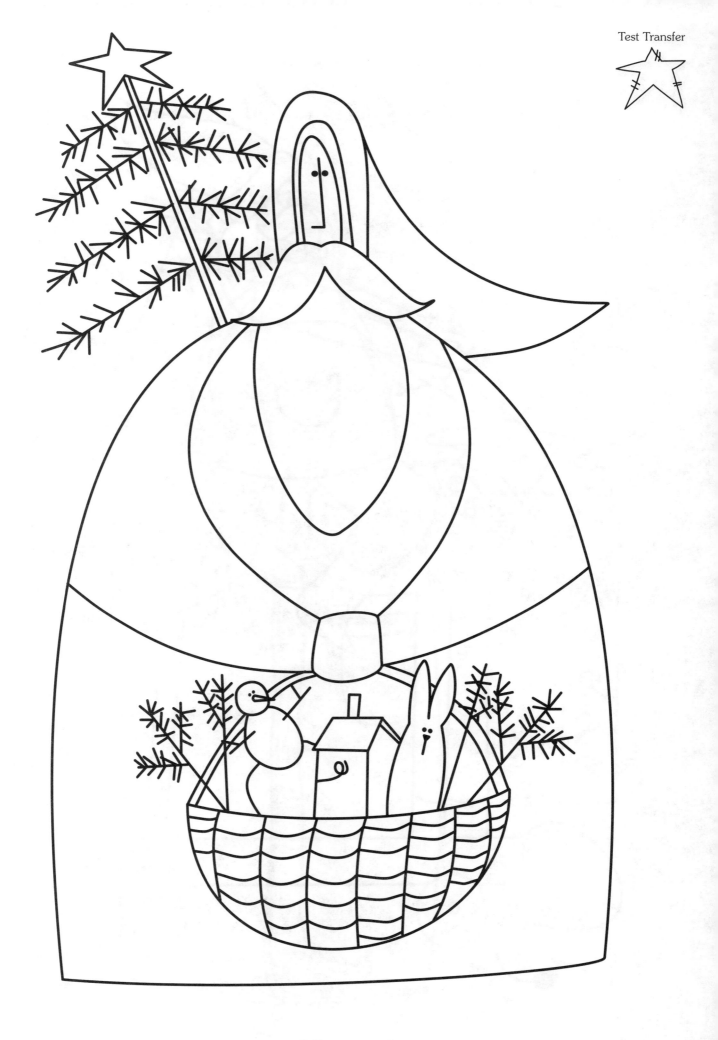

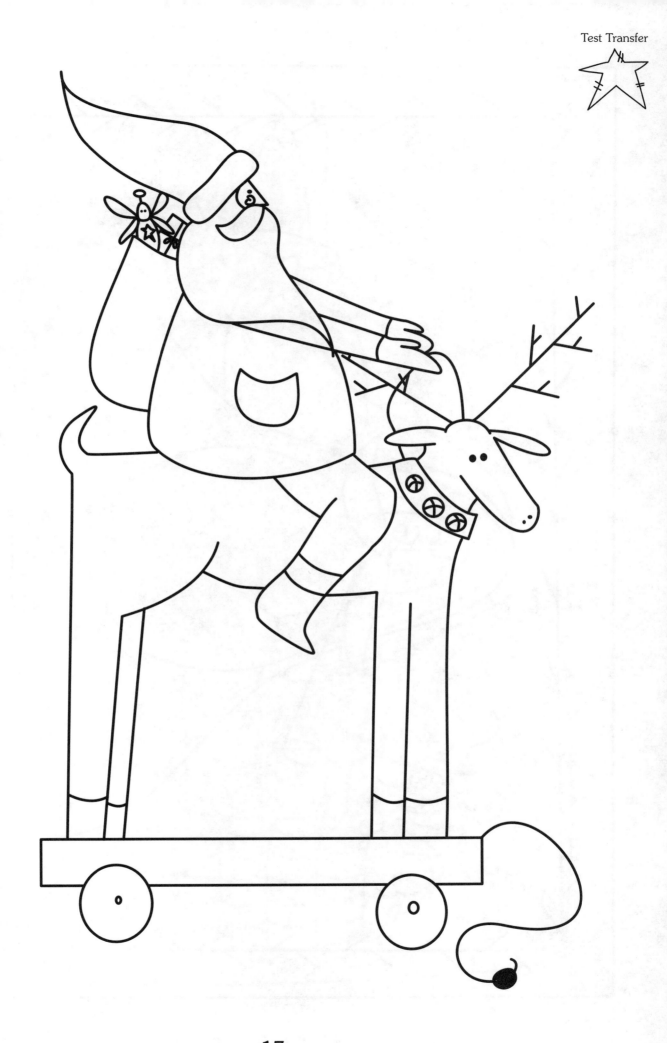

18

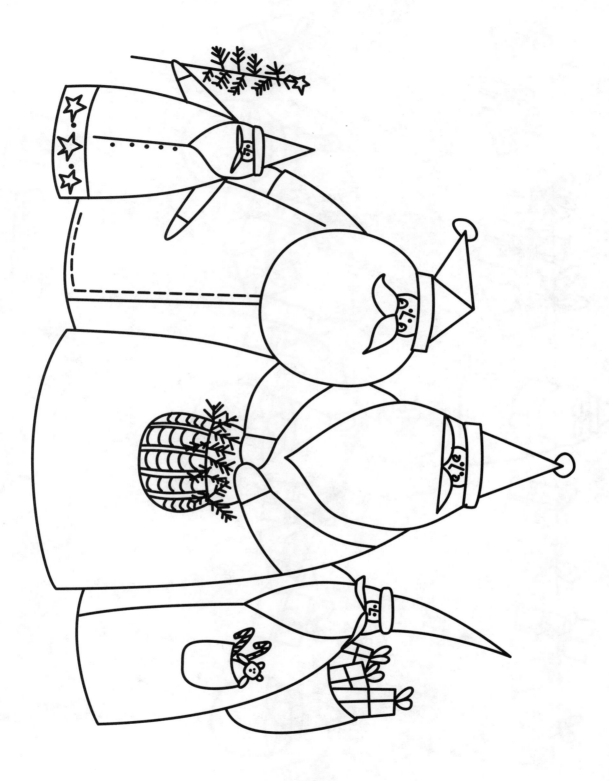

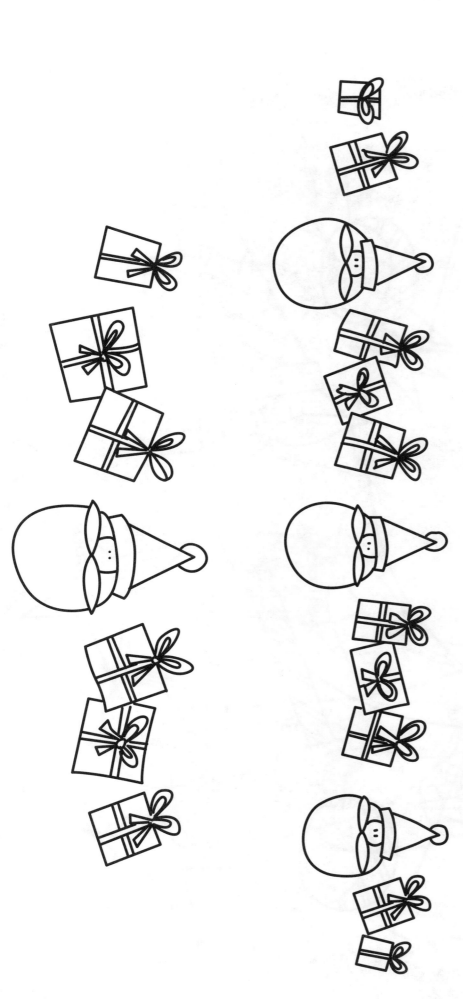

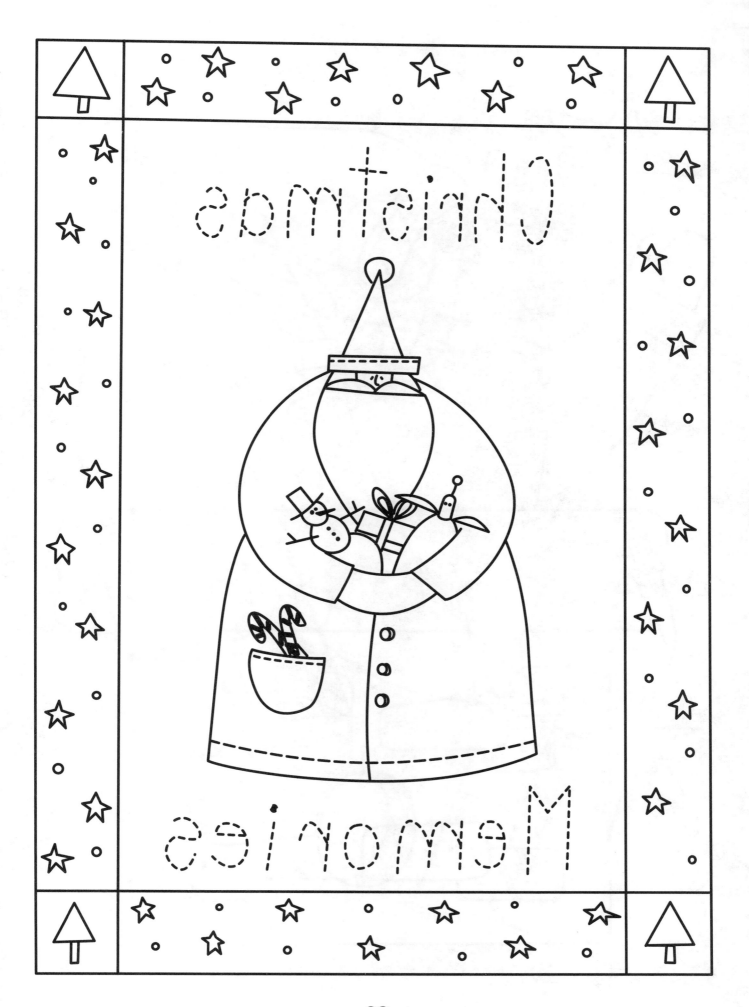

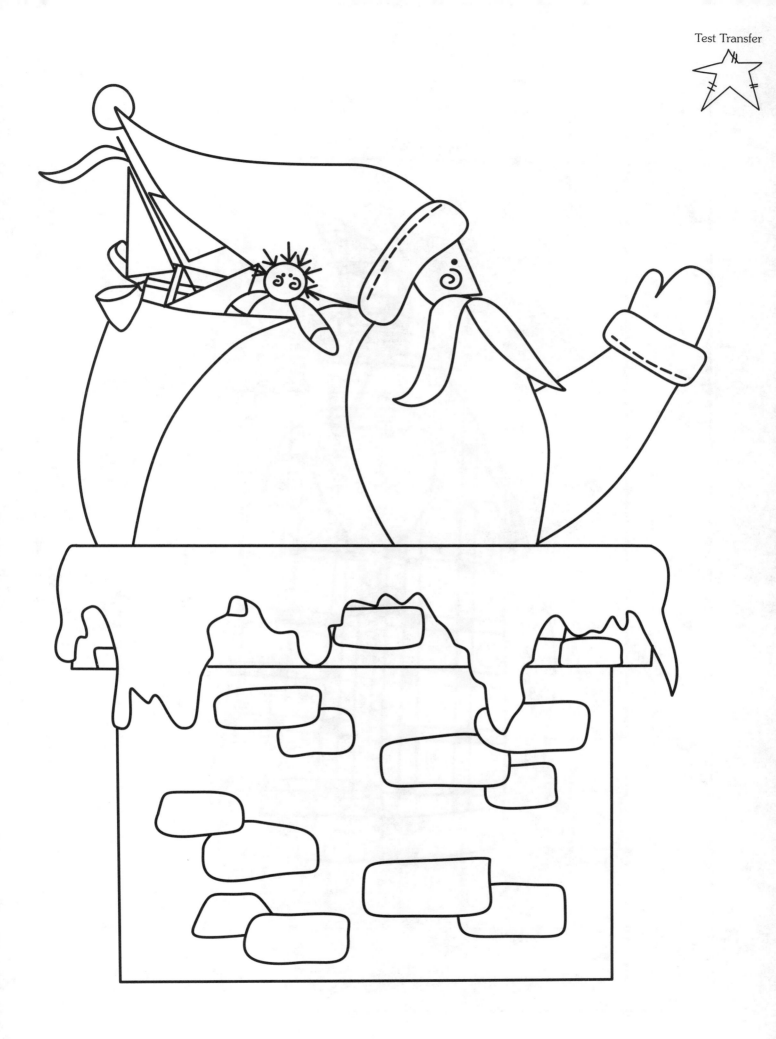

CHRISTMAS
MEMORIES

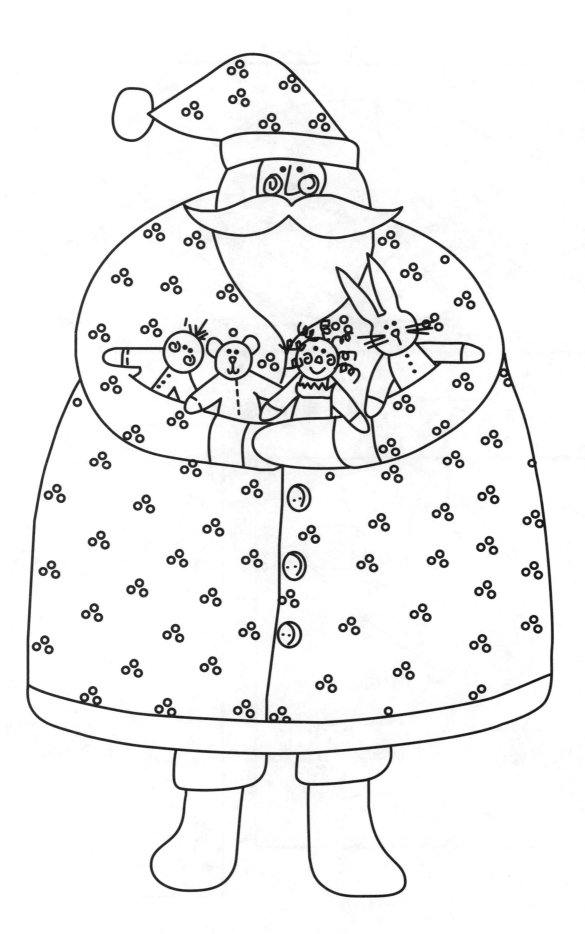

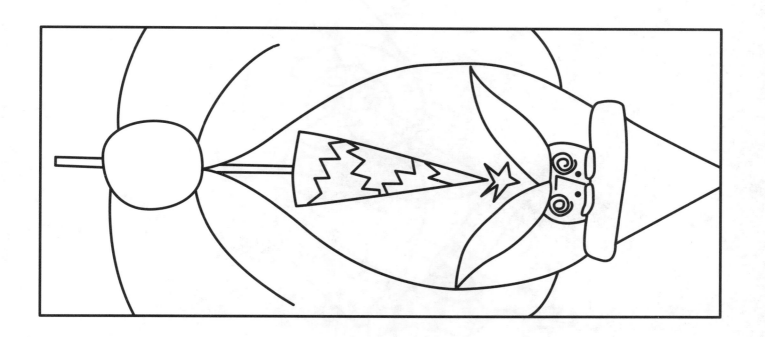

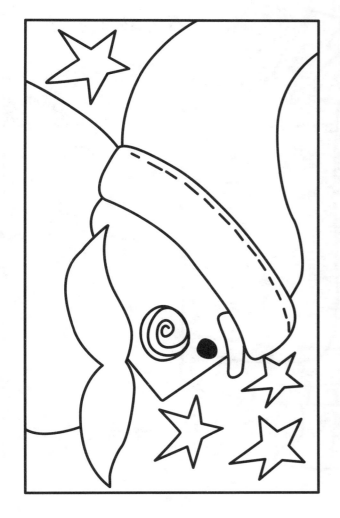

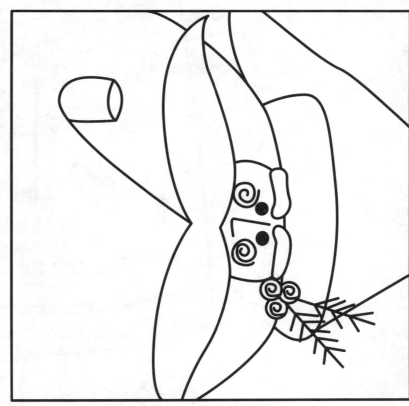

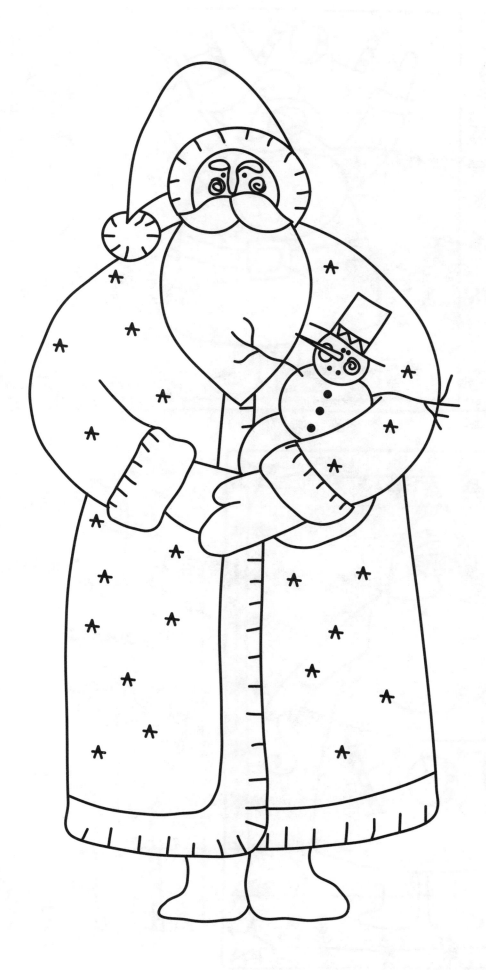

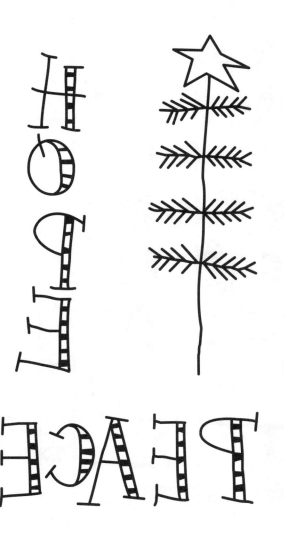

33

34

35

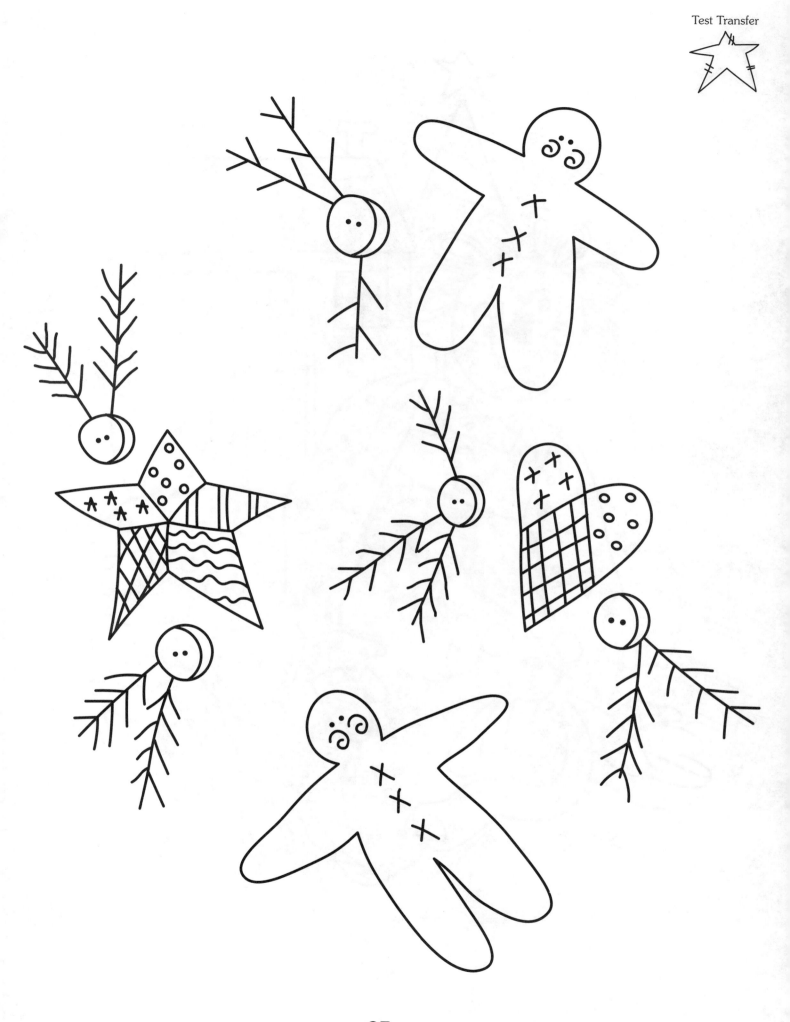

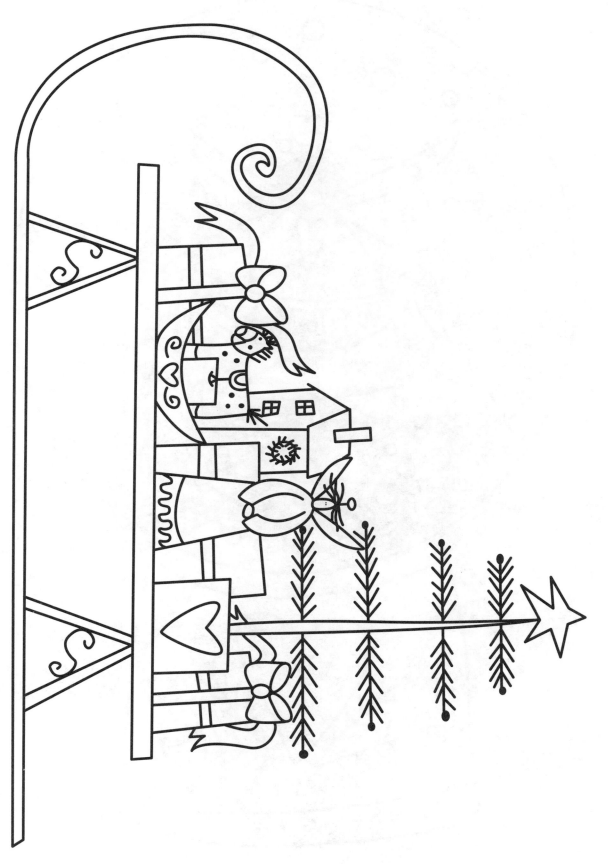

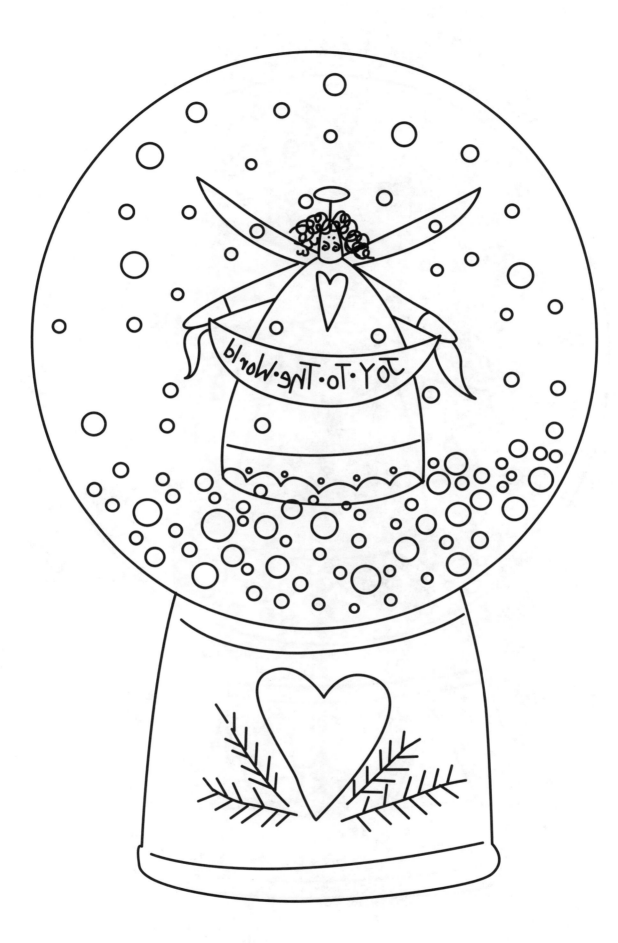

Test Transfer

44

45

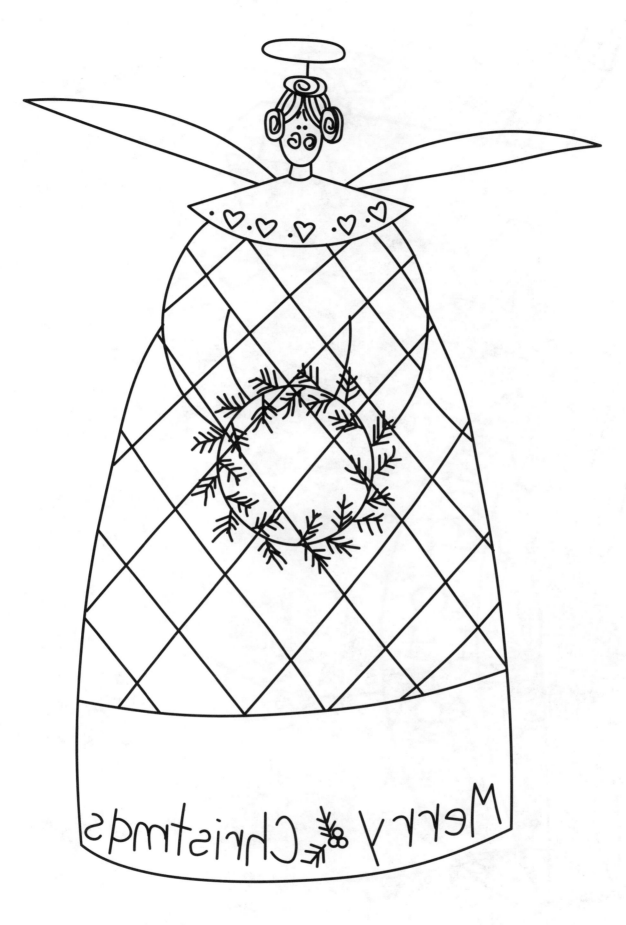

51

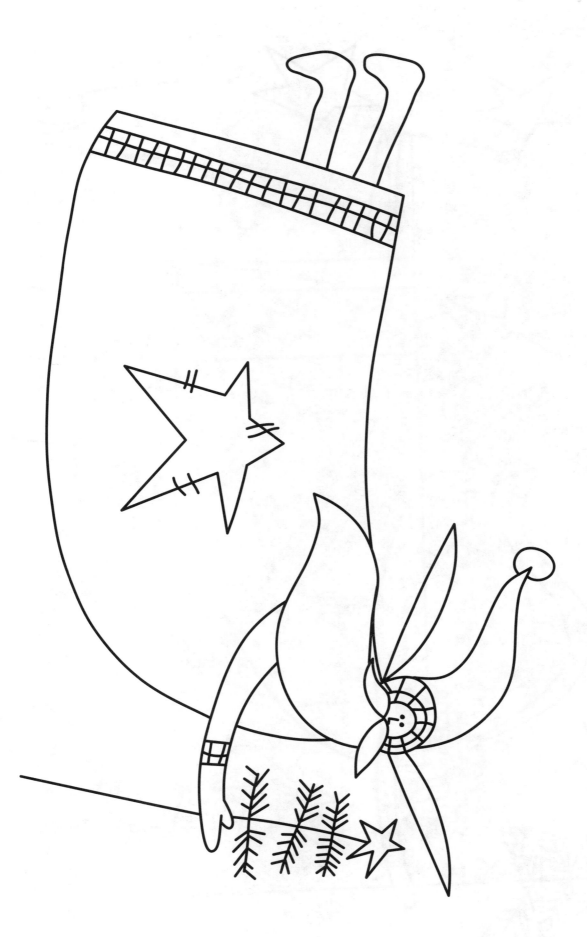

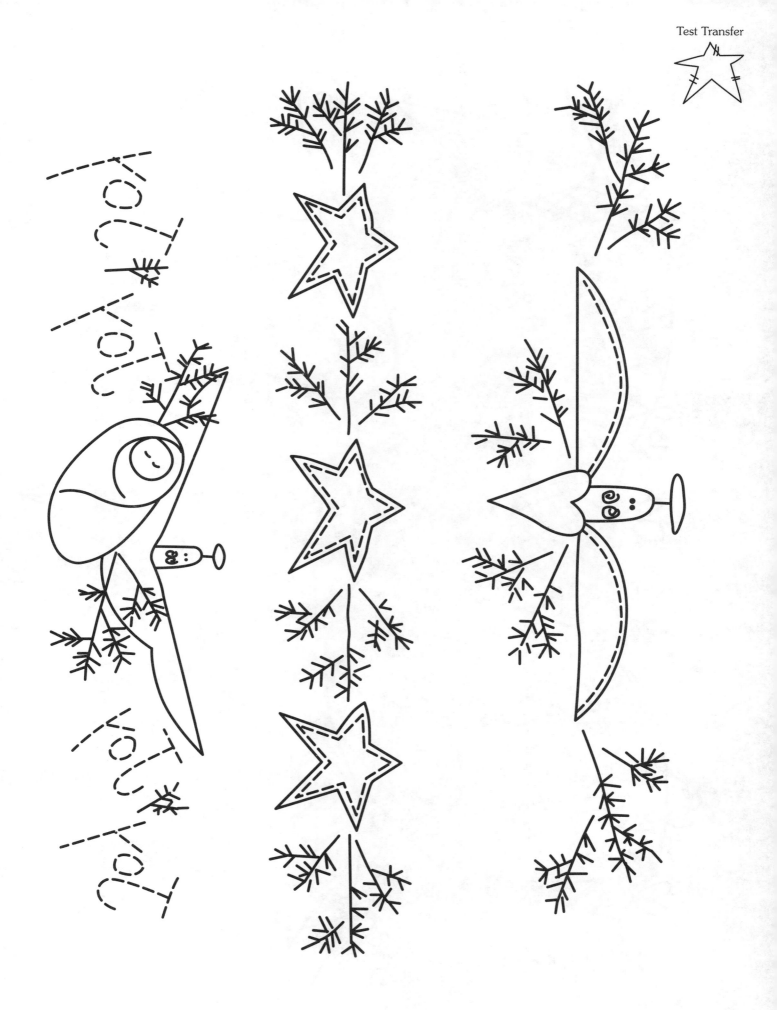

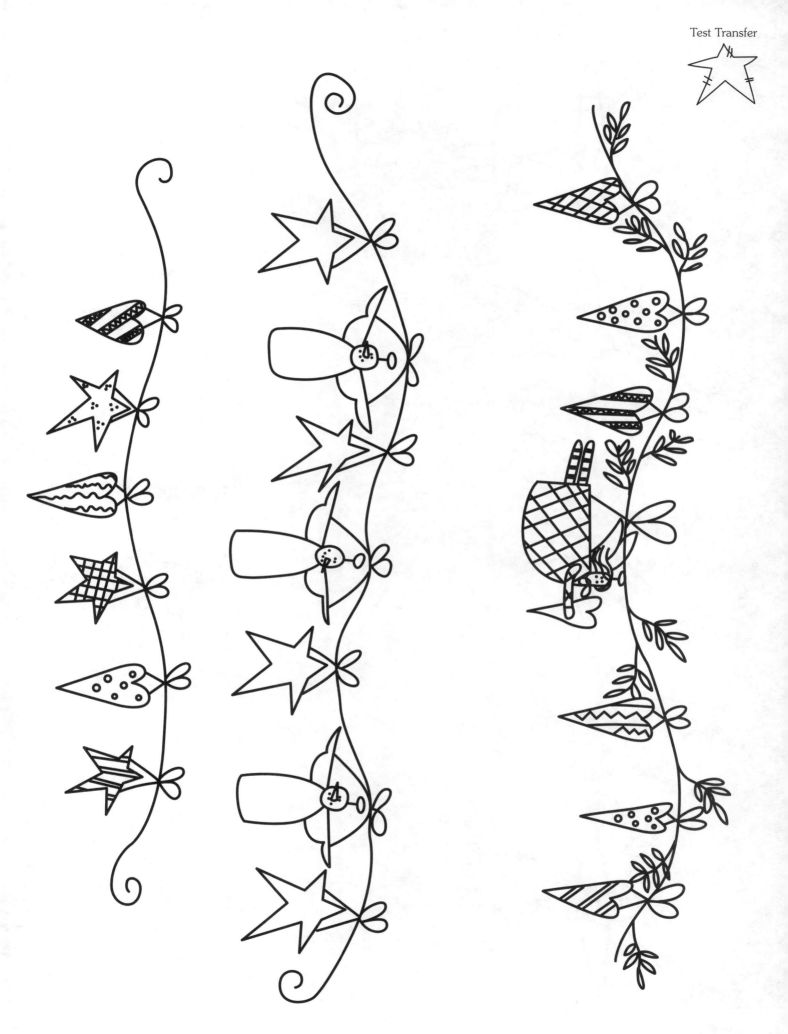

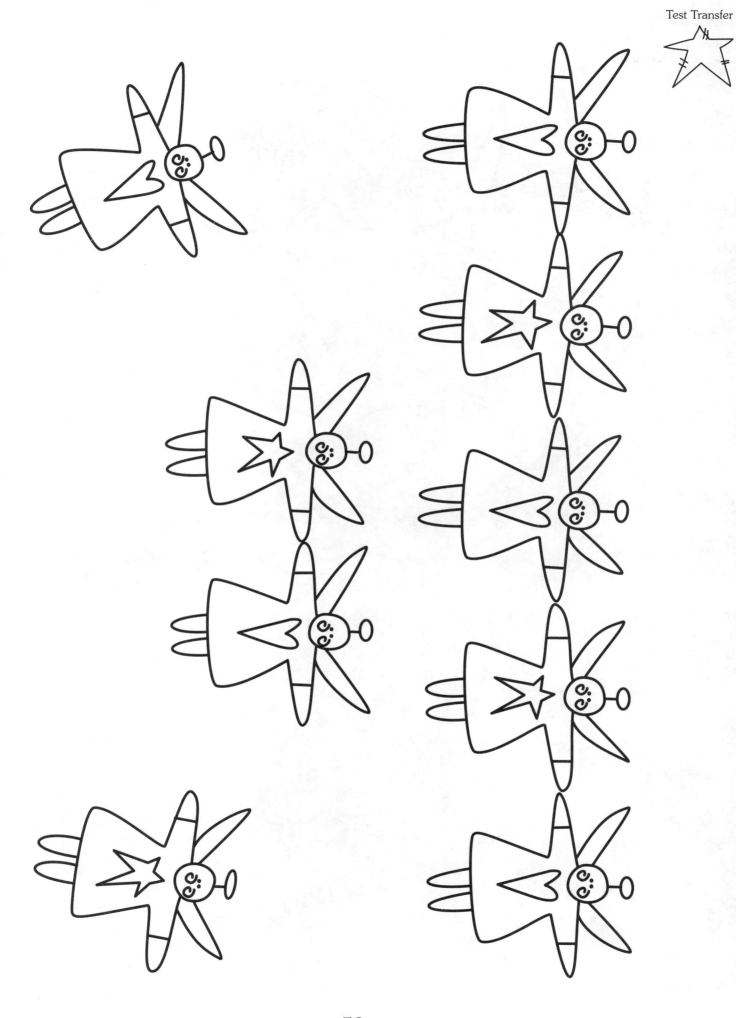

59

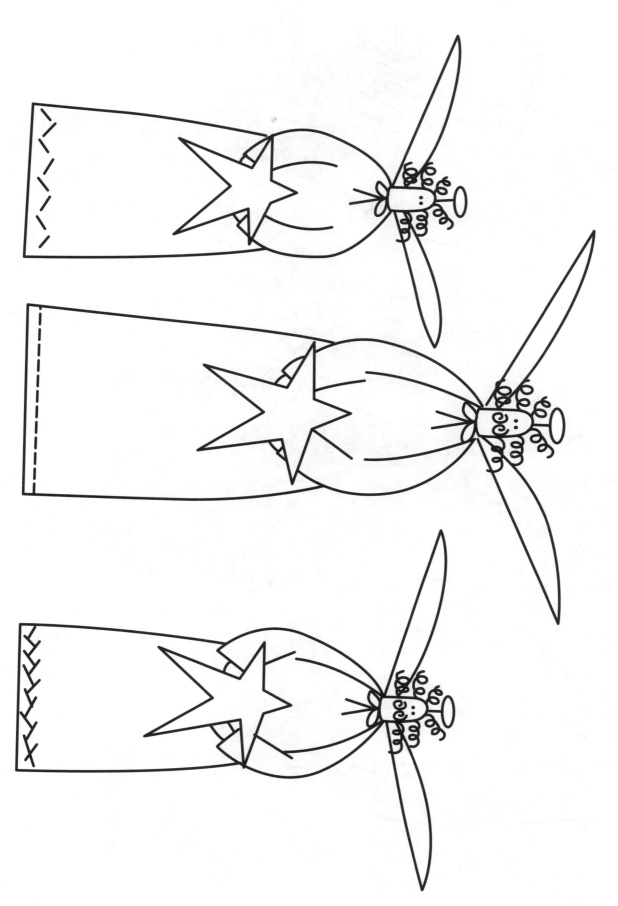

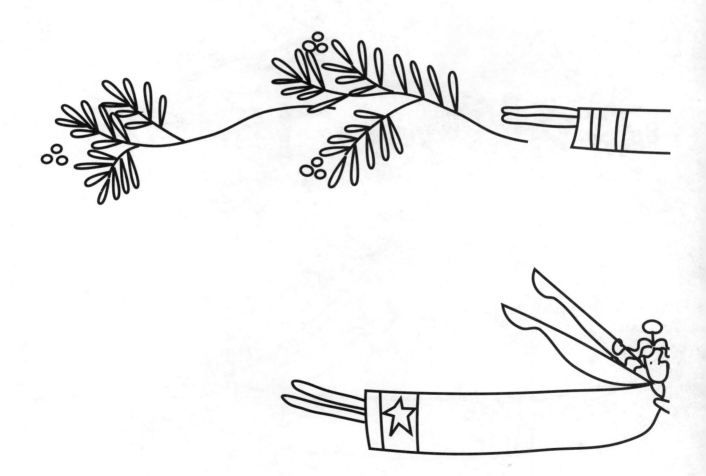

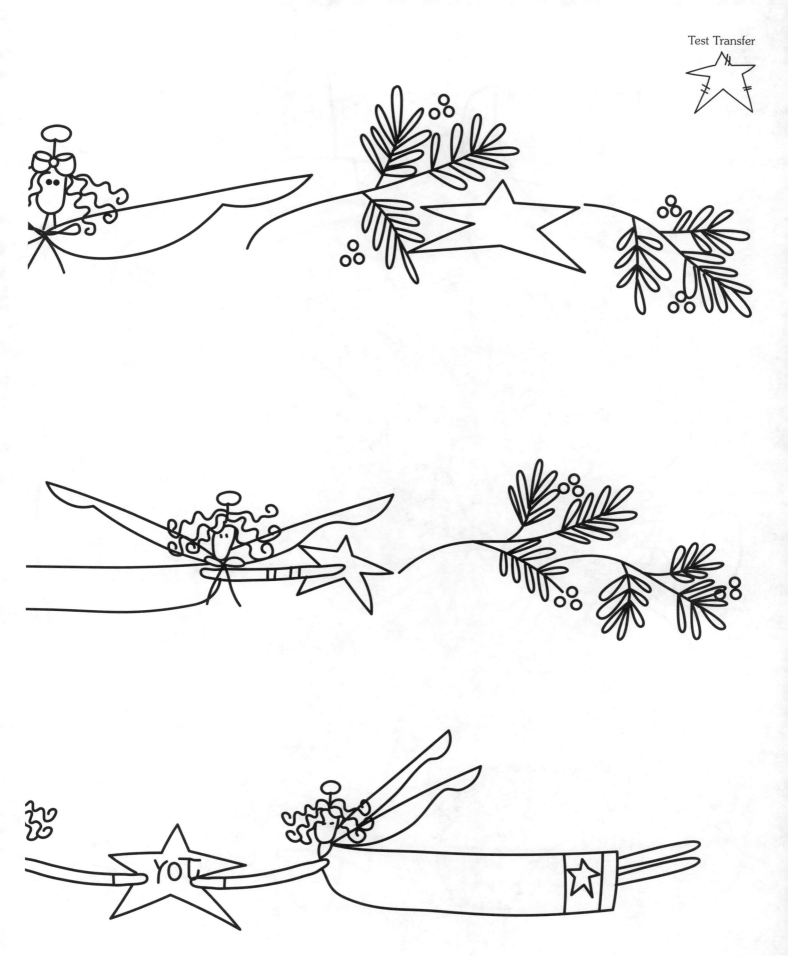

65

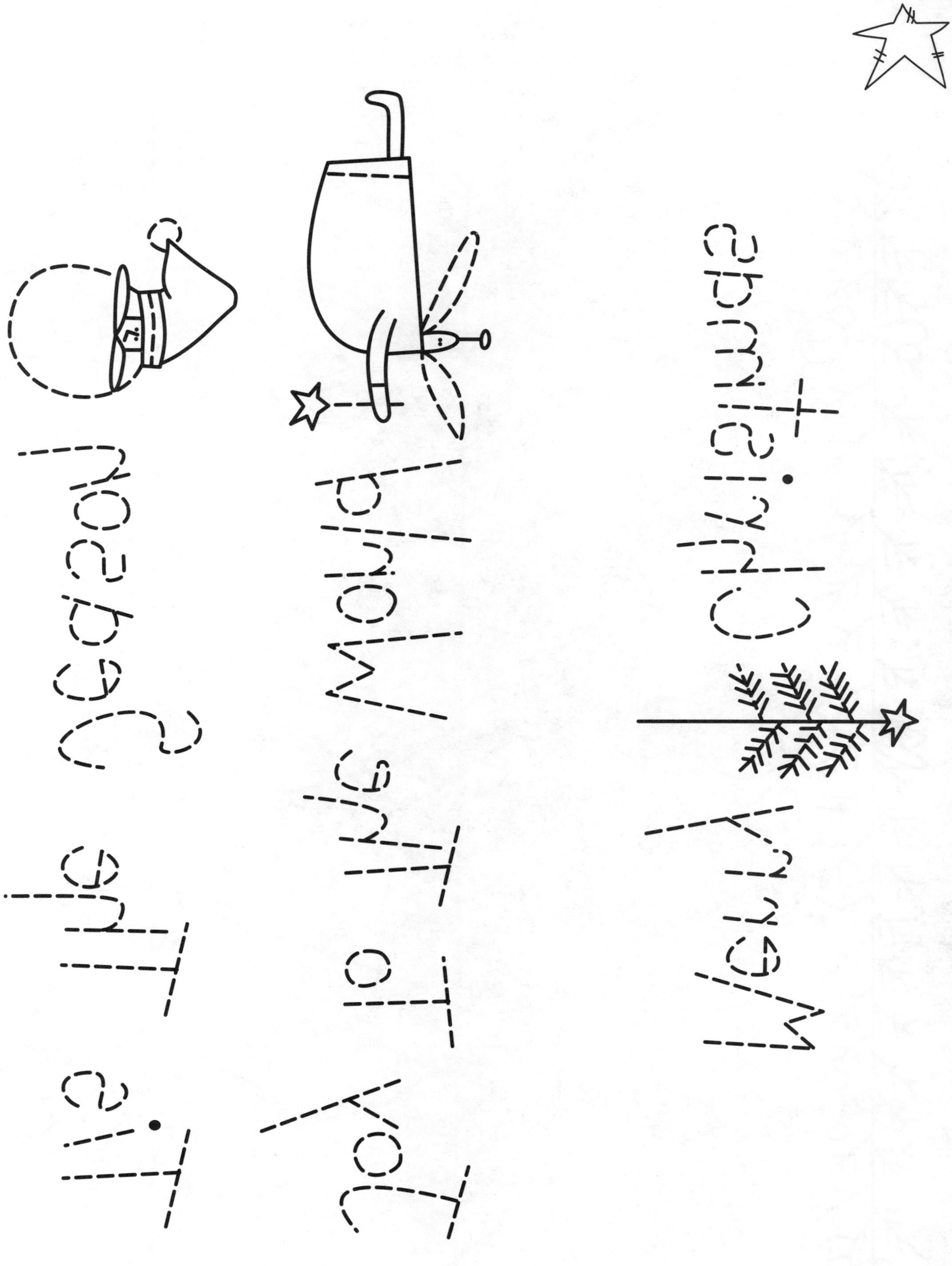

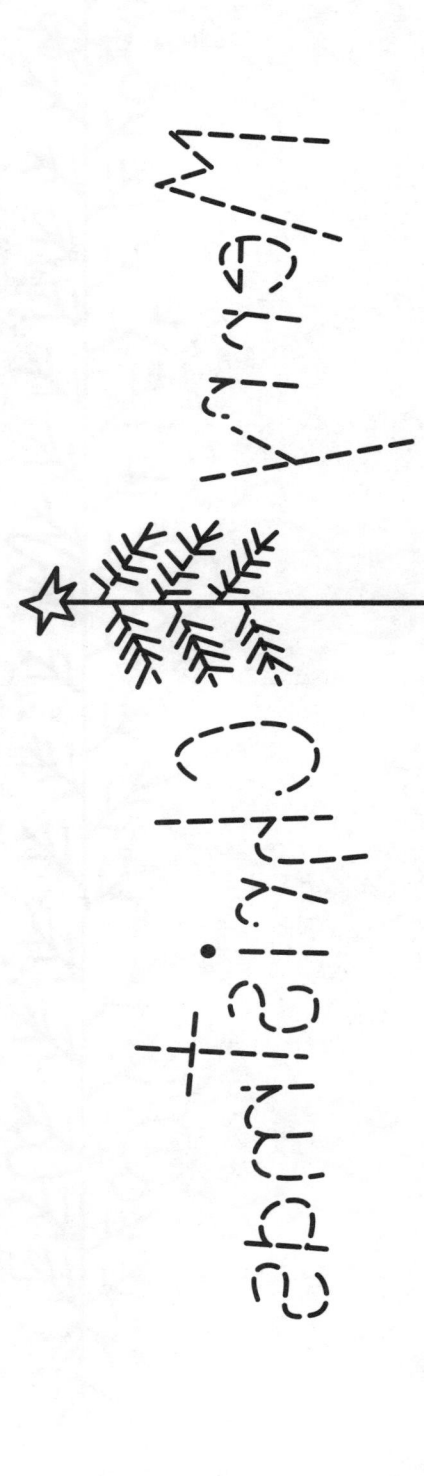

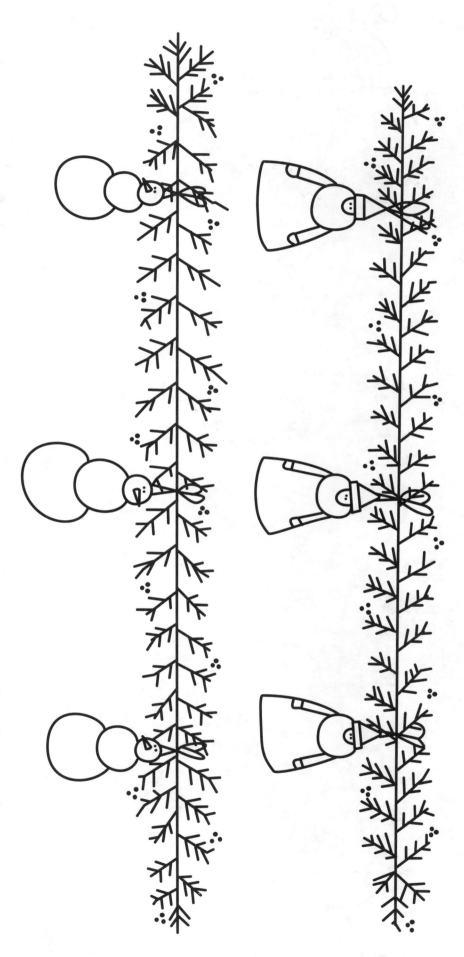

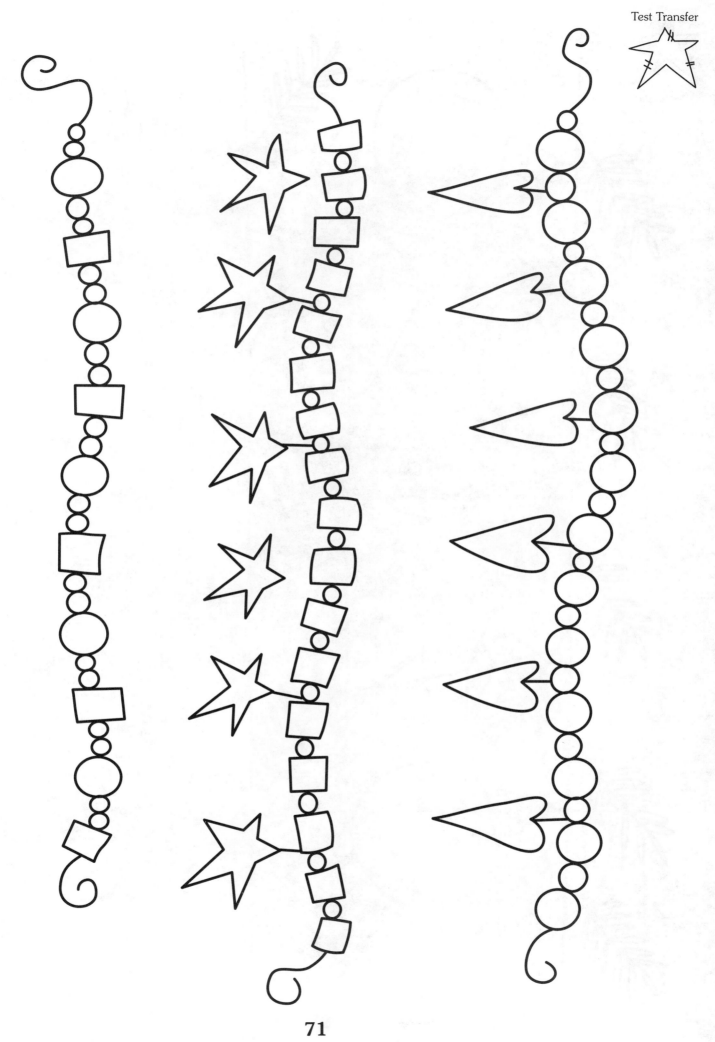

71

72

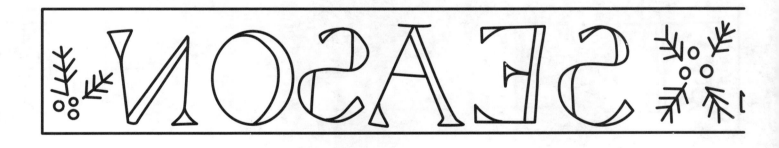

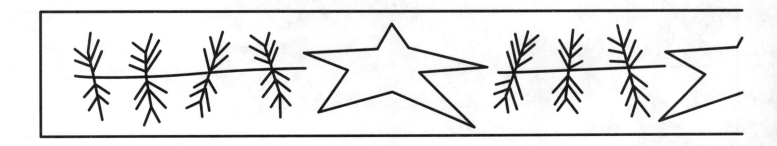

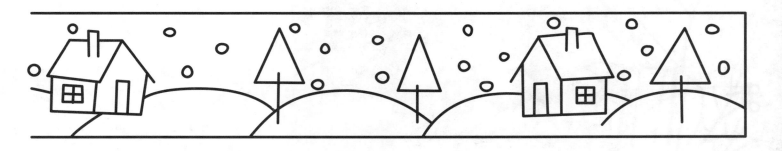

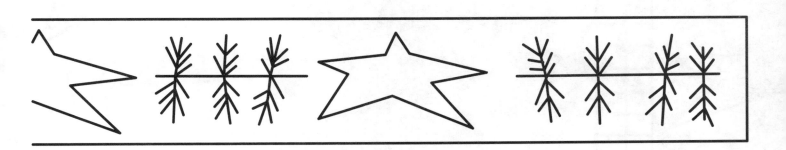

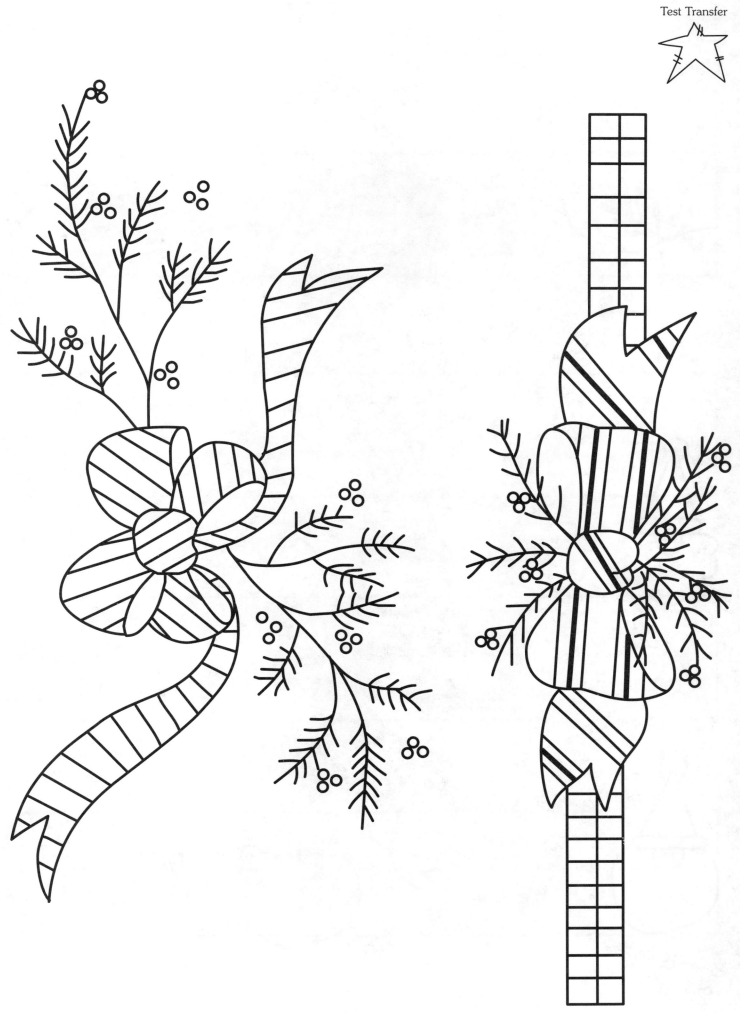

75

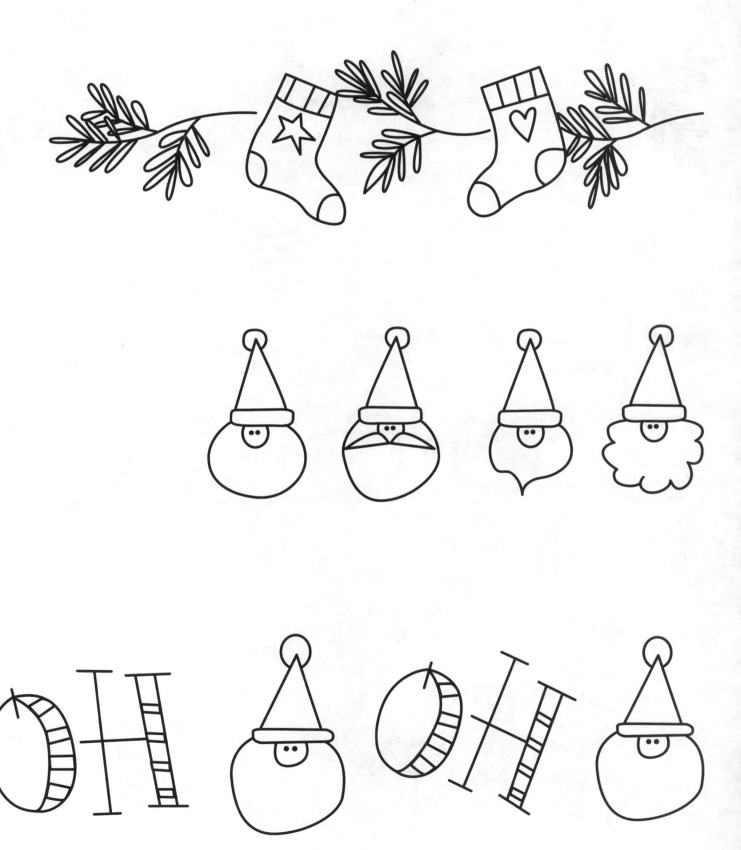

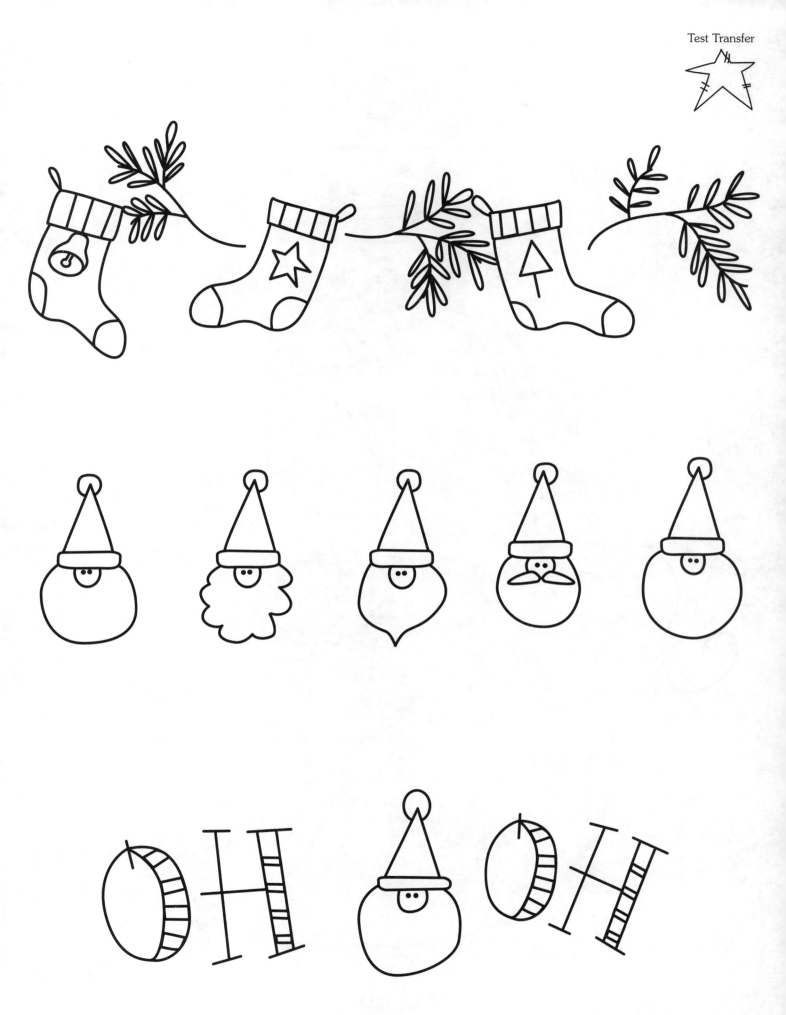

77

81

Catch A Falling Star

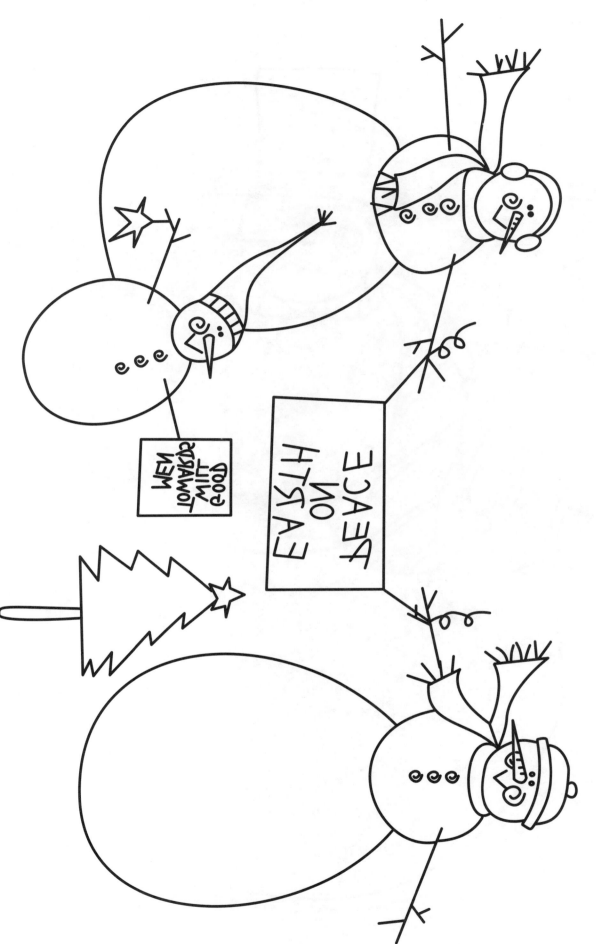

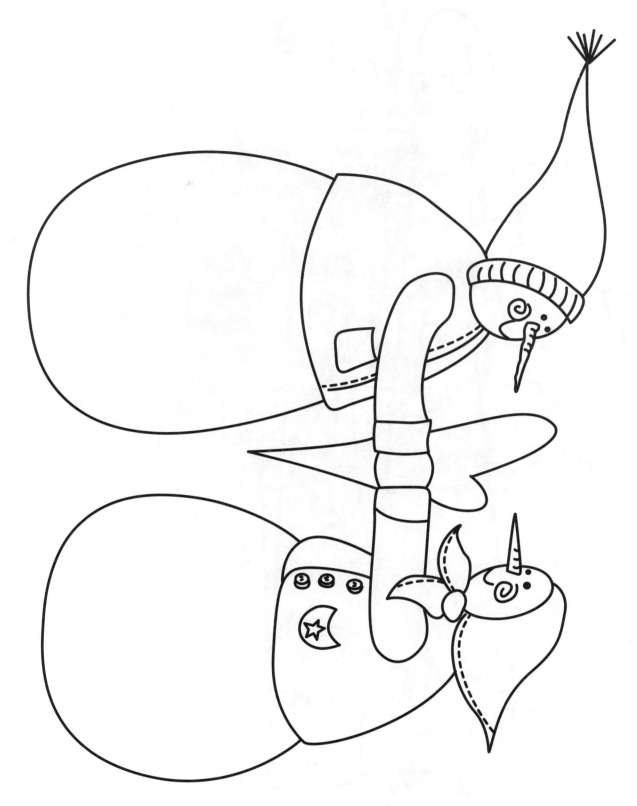

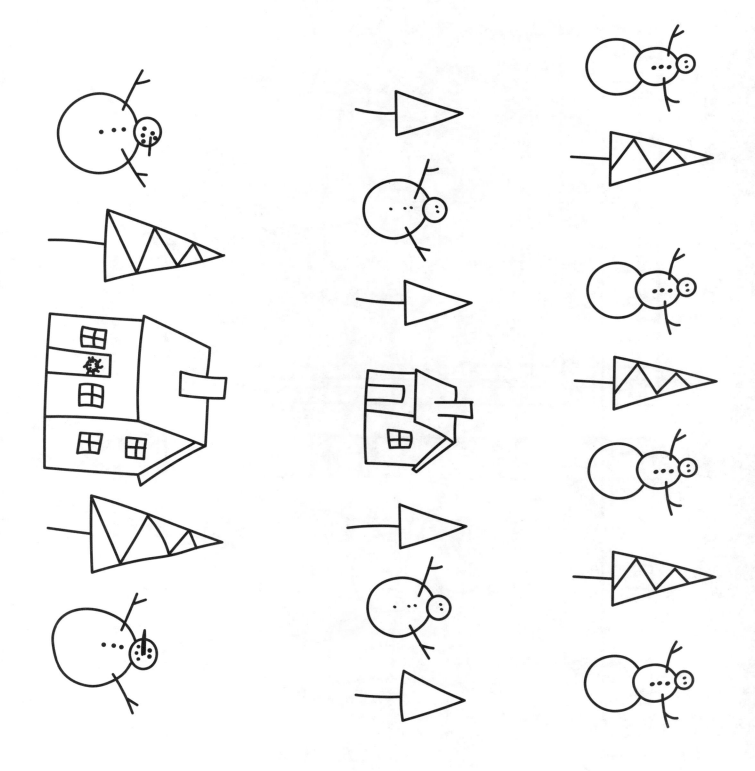

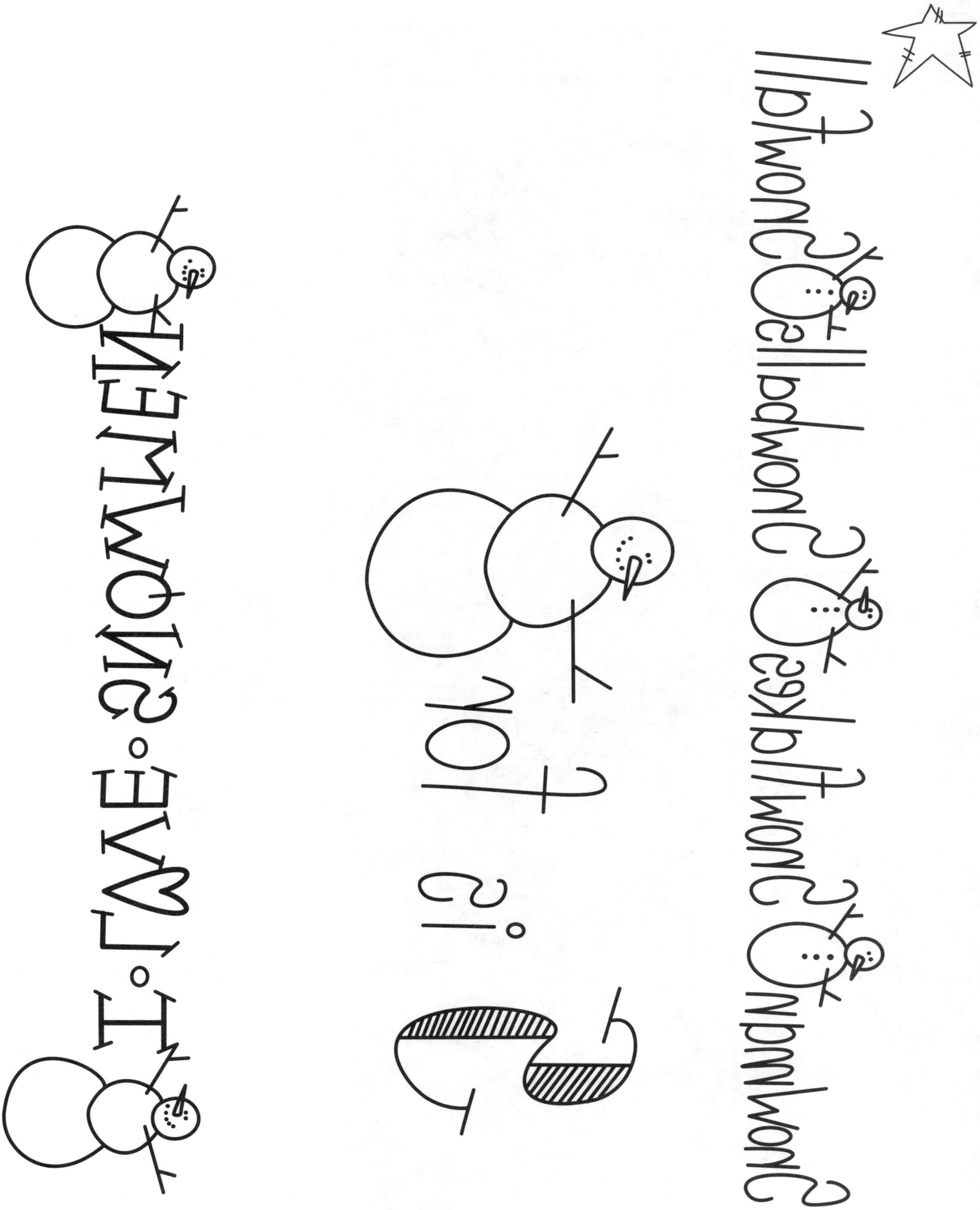
I·LOVE·SNOWMEN
Snowman Snowflake Snowball

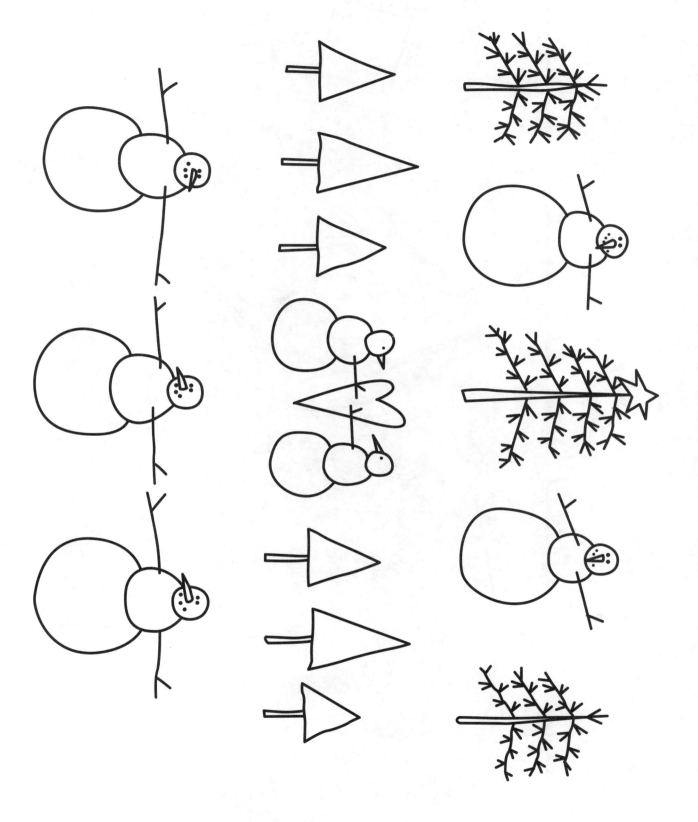

Test Transfer

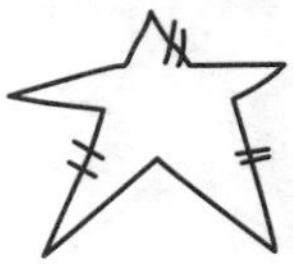

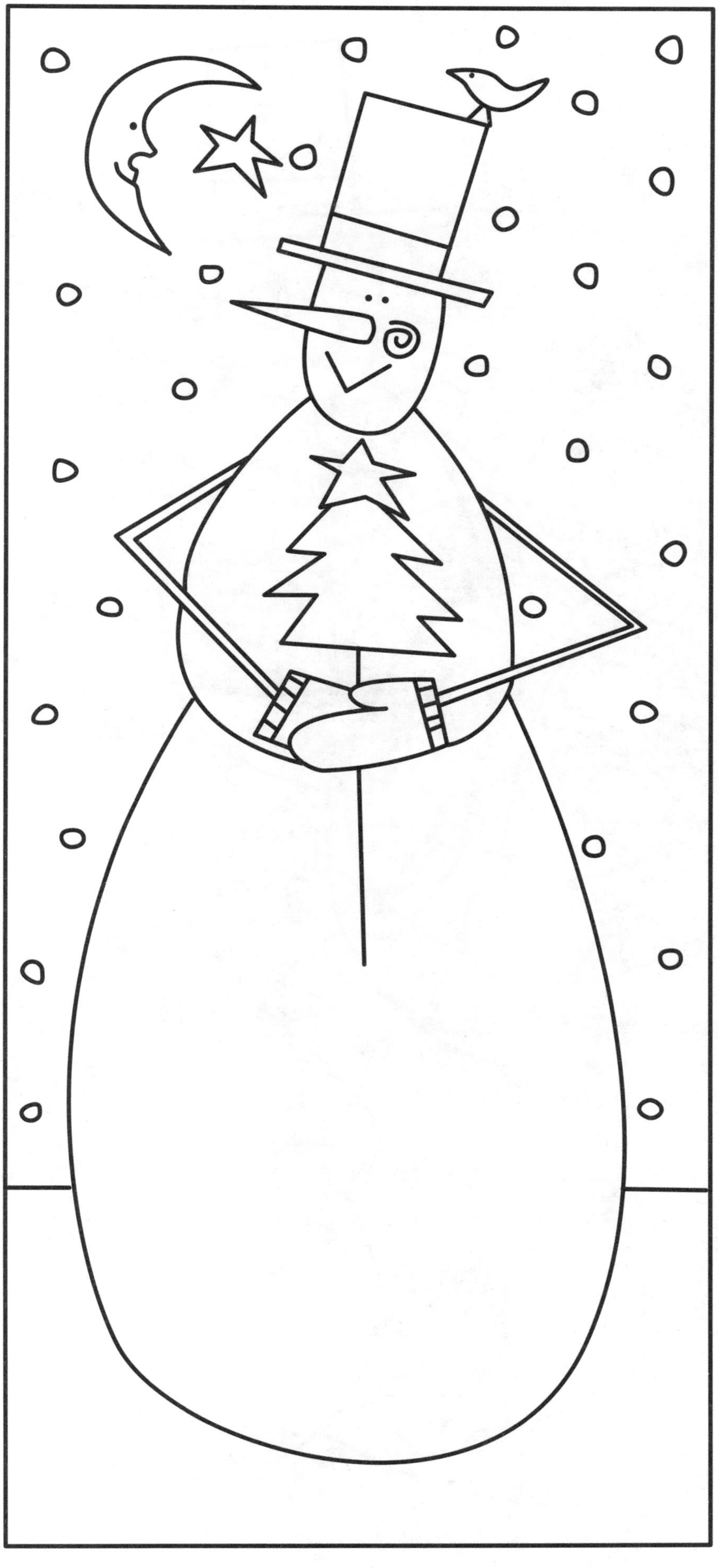

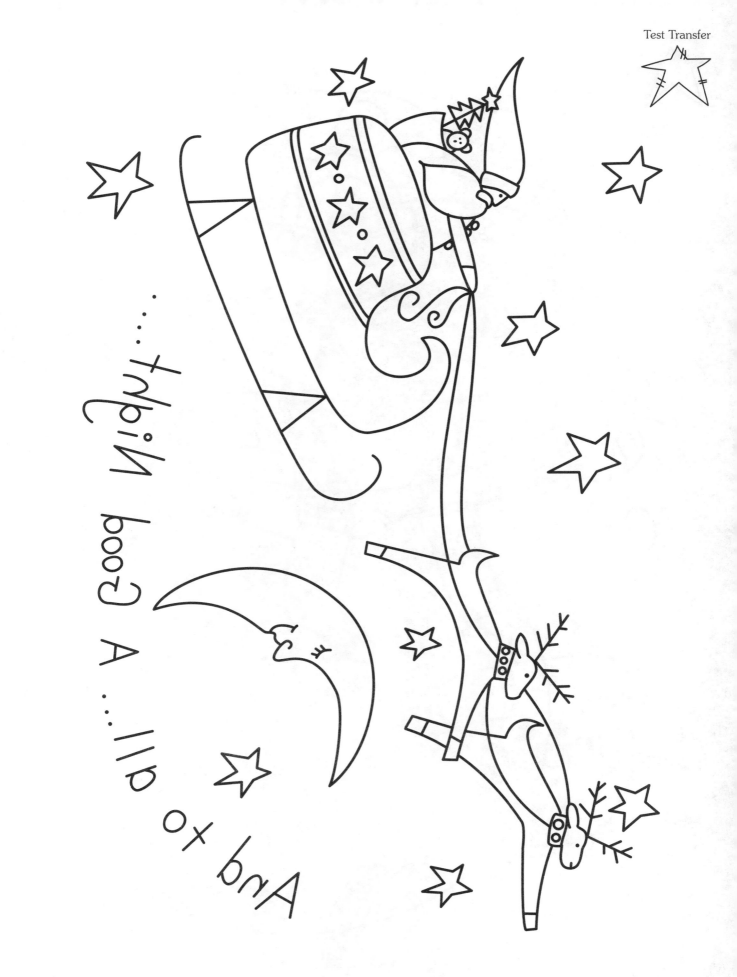

And to all ... A ... Good Night ...

98

101

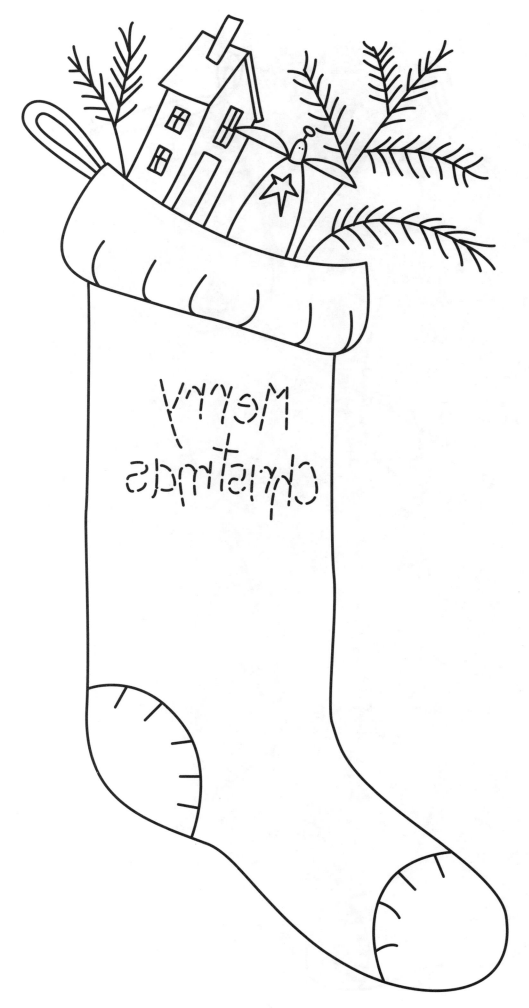

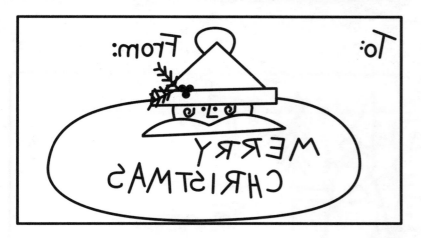

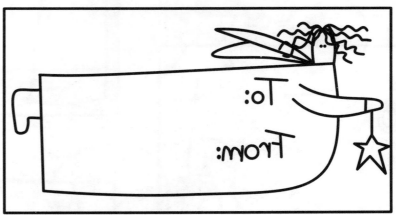

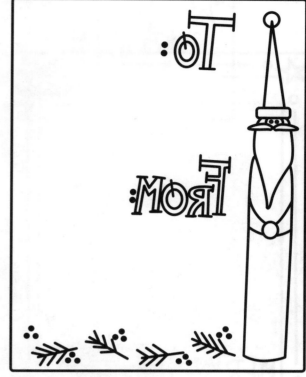

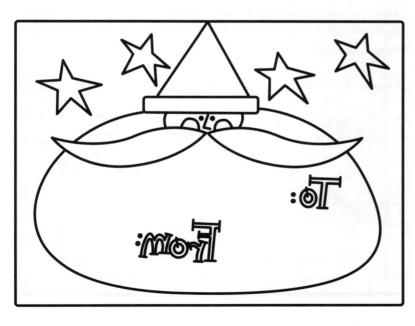

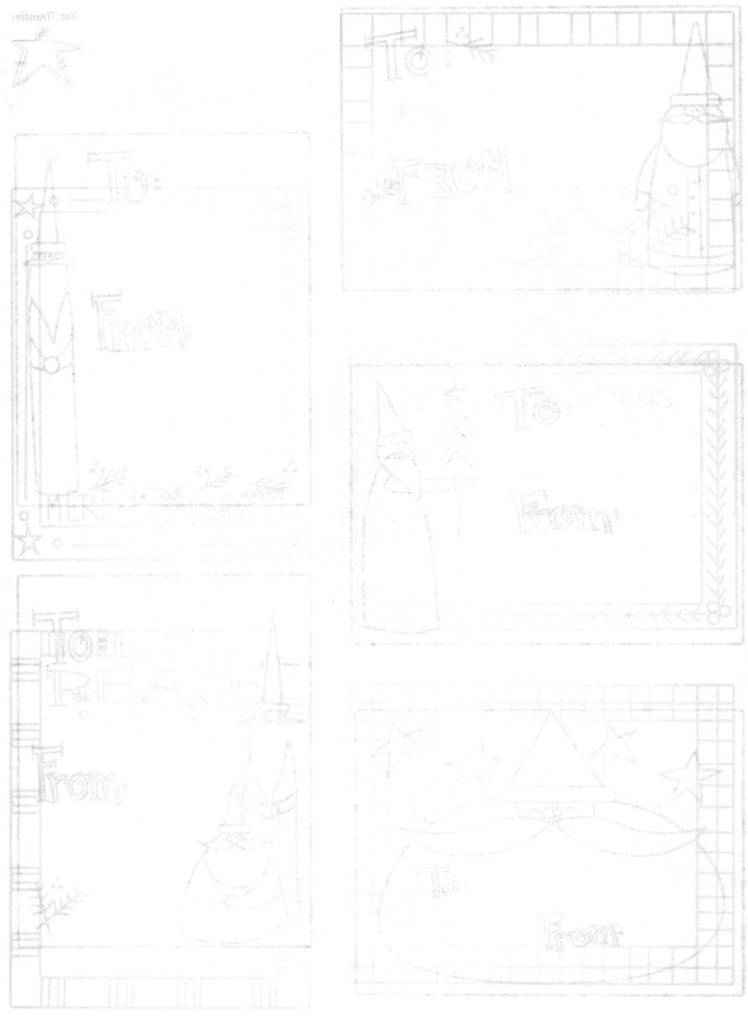

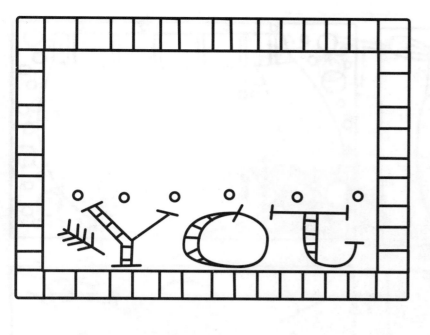

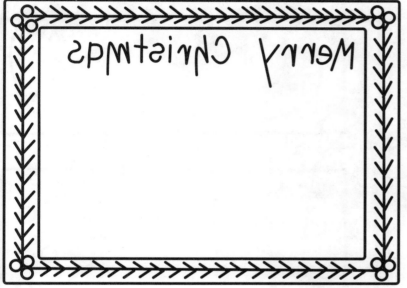

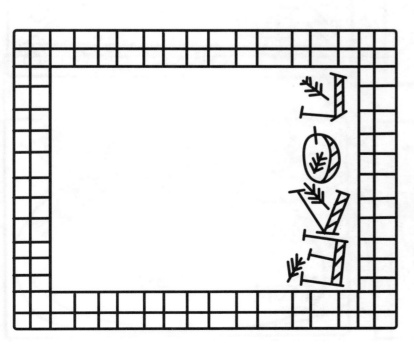

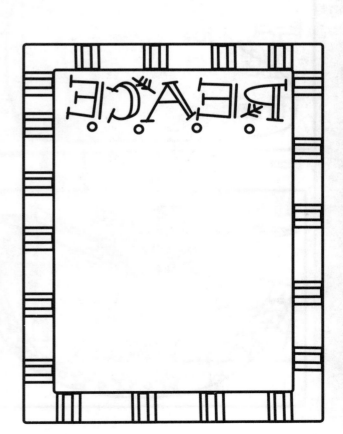

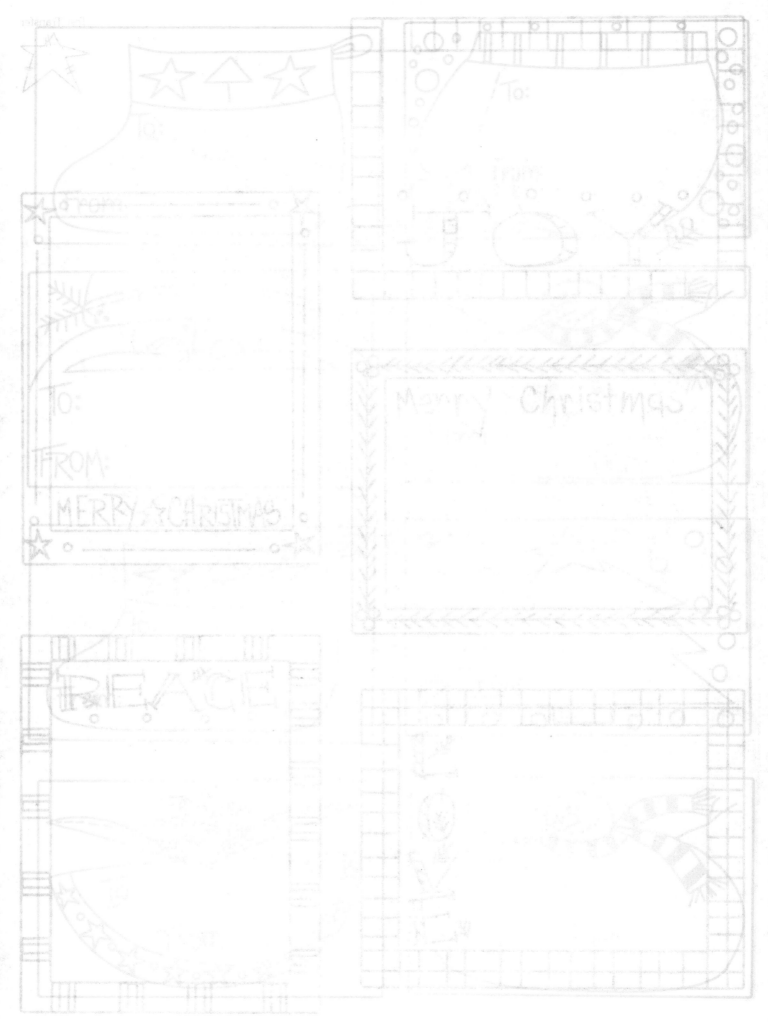

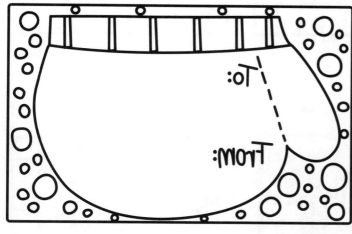

To:

From:

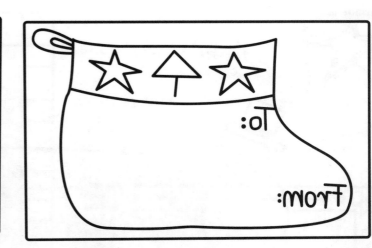

To:

From:

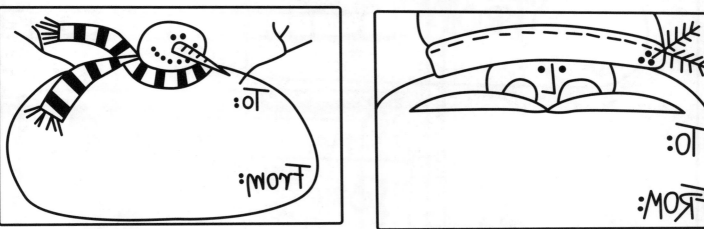

To:

FROM:

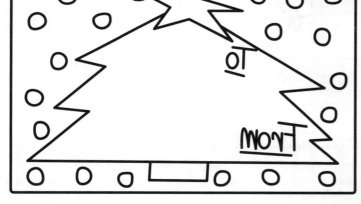

To:

From:

To:

From:

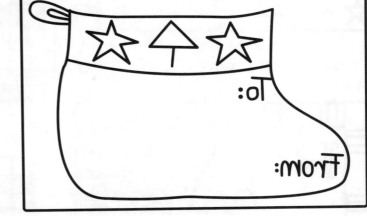

To:

From:

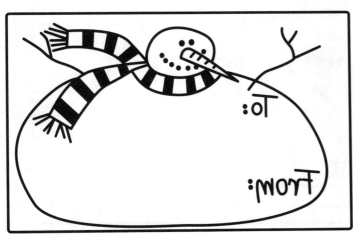

To:

From:

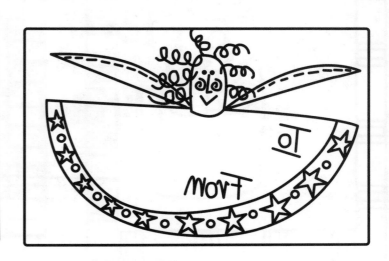

To:

From:

114

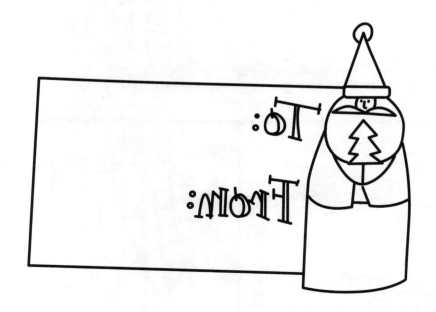

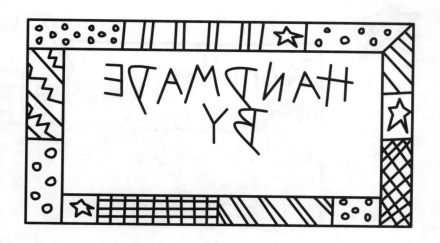

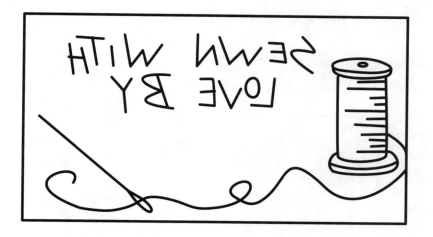

From the
House of

From the
Kitchen
of...

Homemade by.....

From the
House of

From the
Kitchen
of

Homemade by...

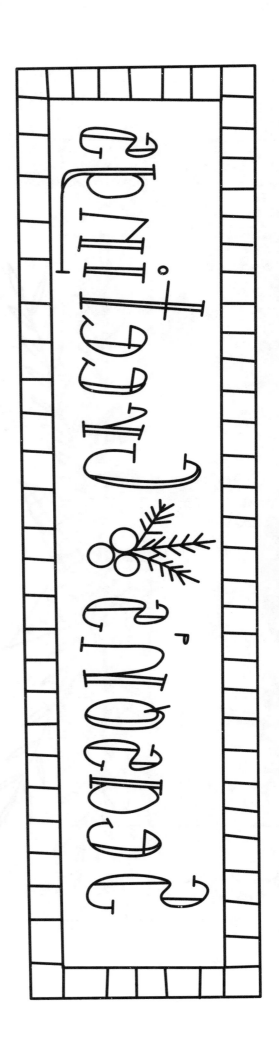

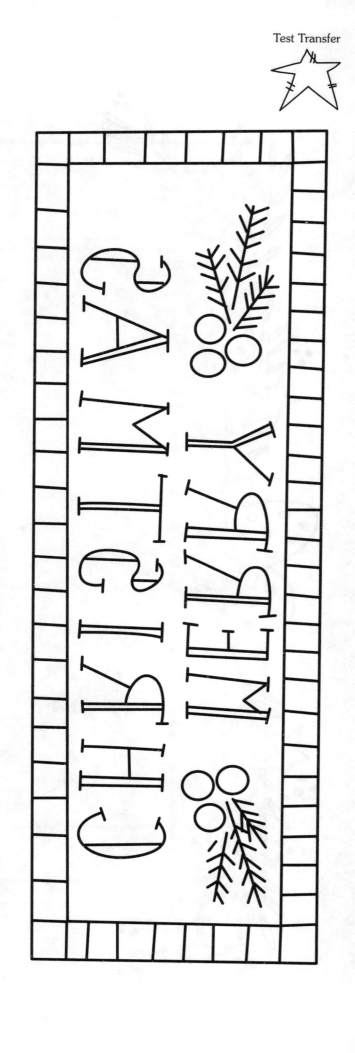

121

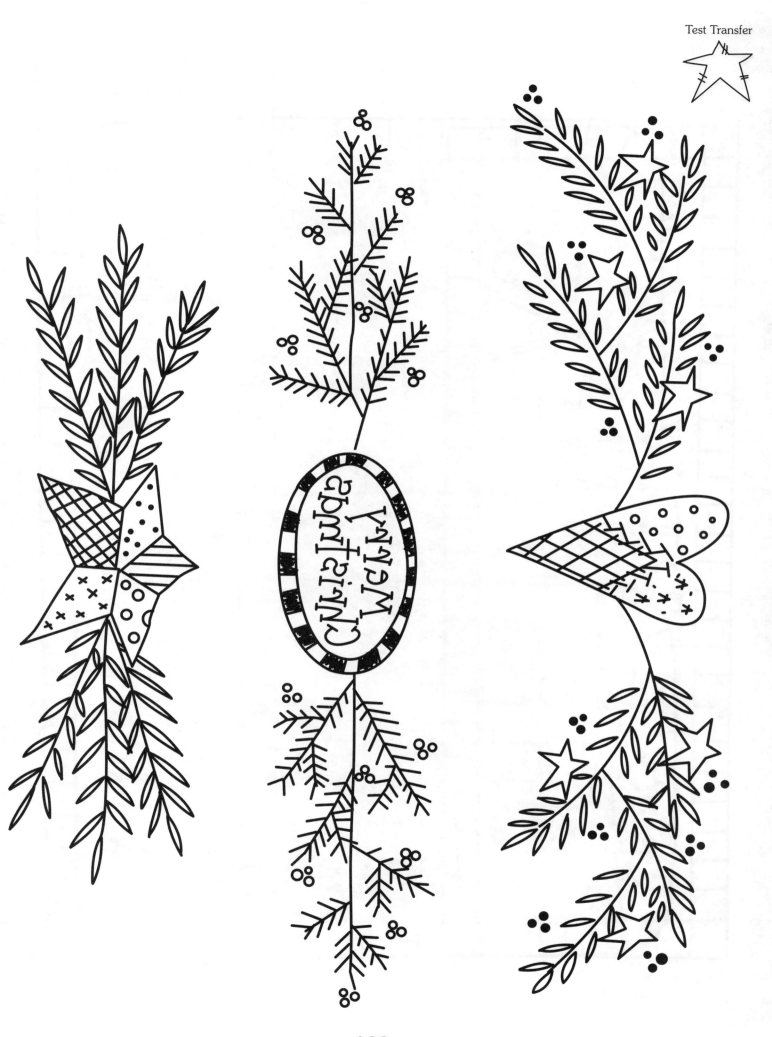

Merry
Christmas

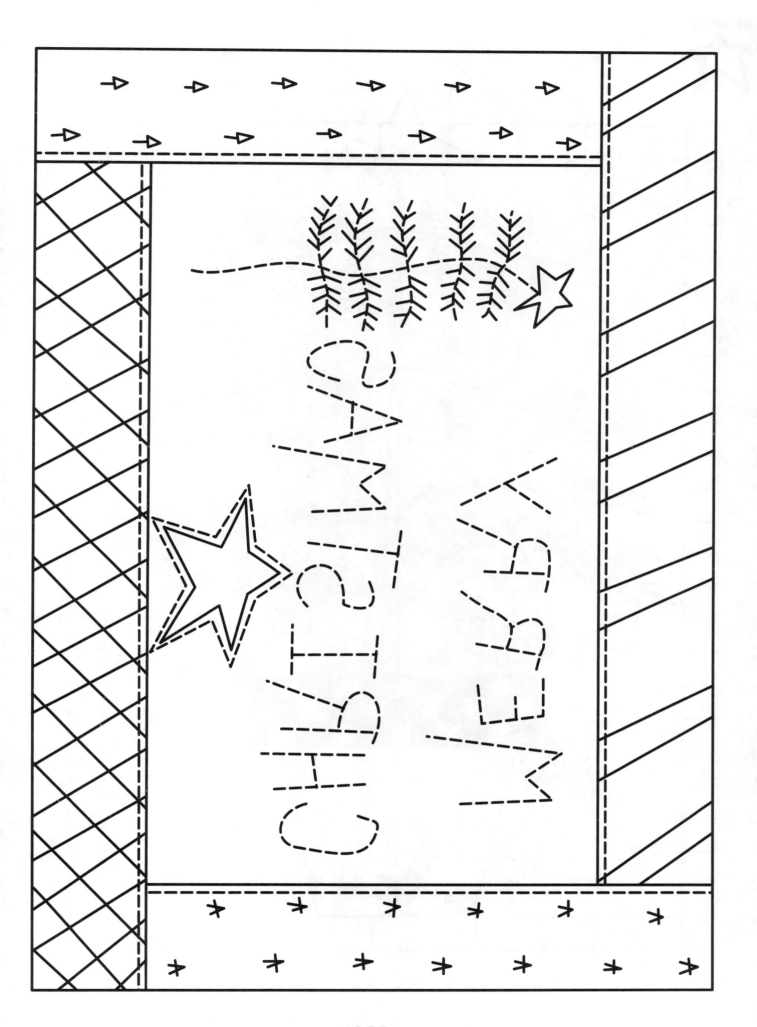

125

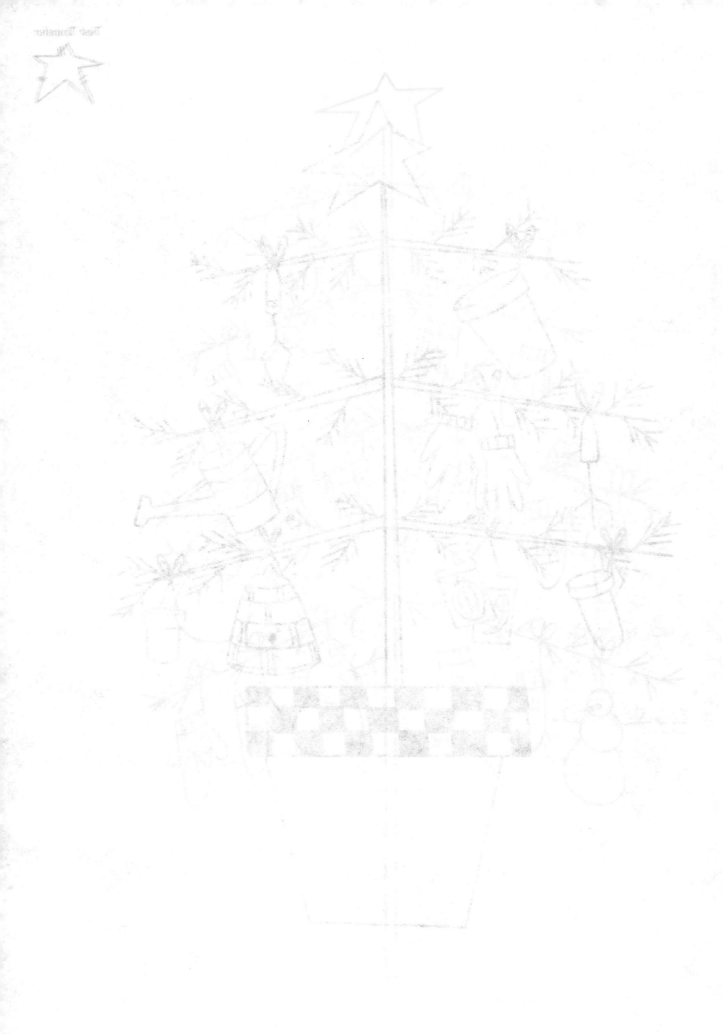

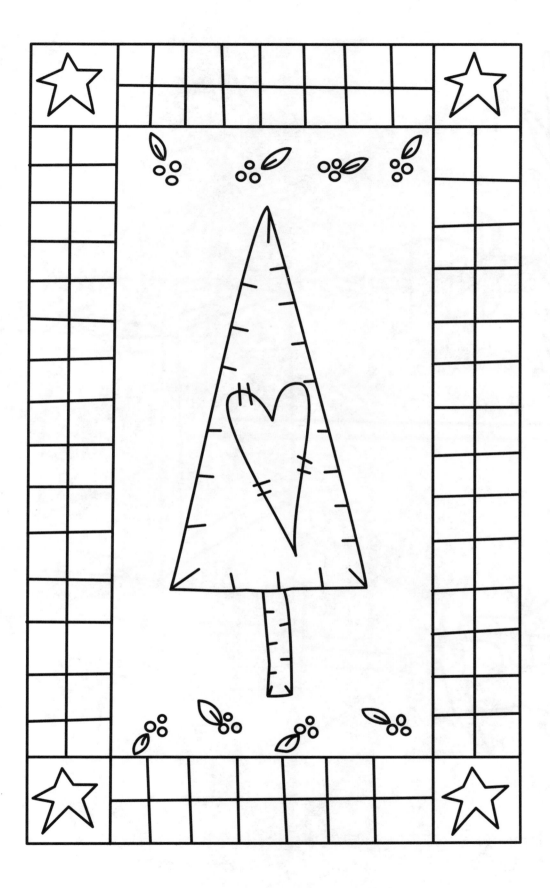

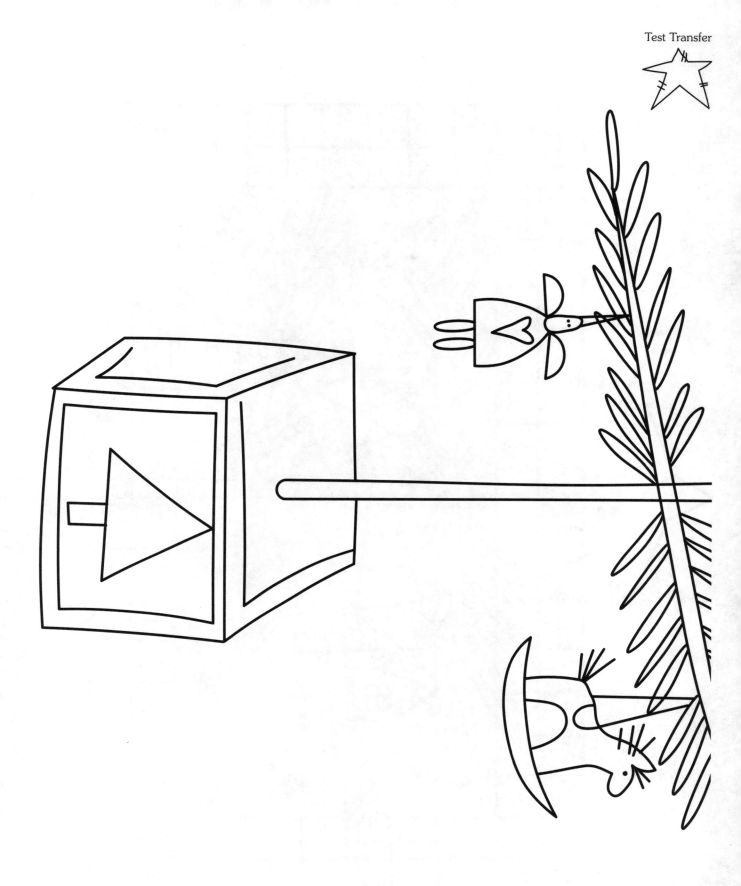

130

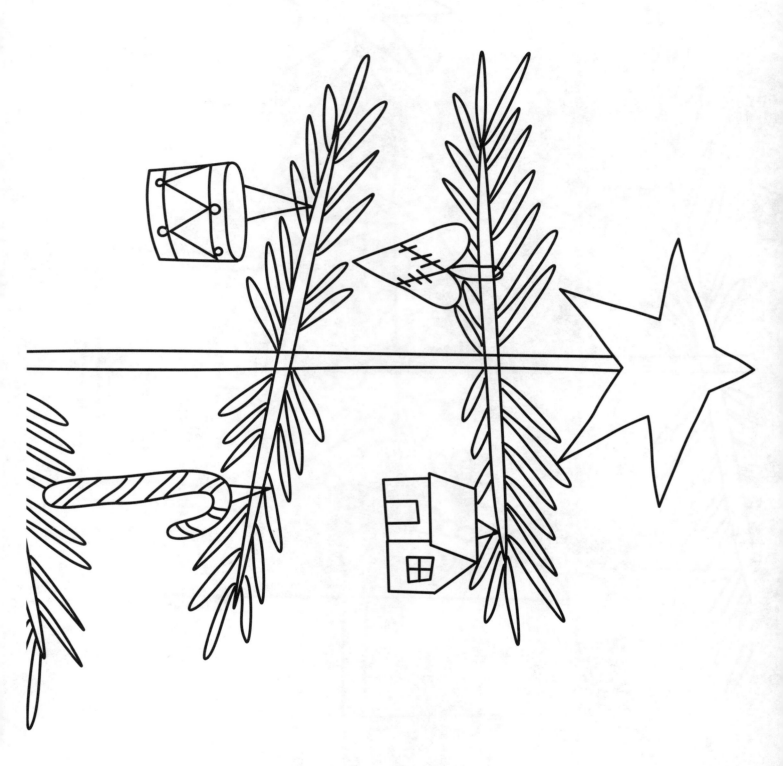

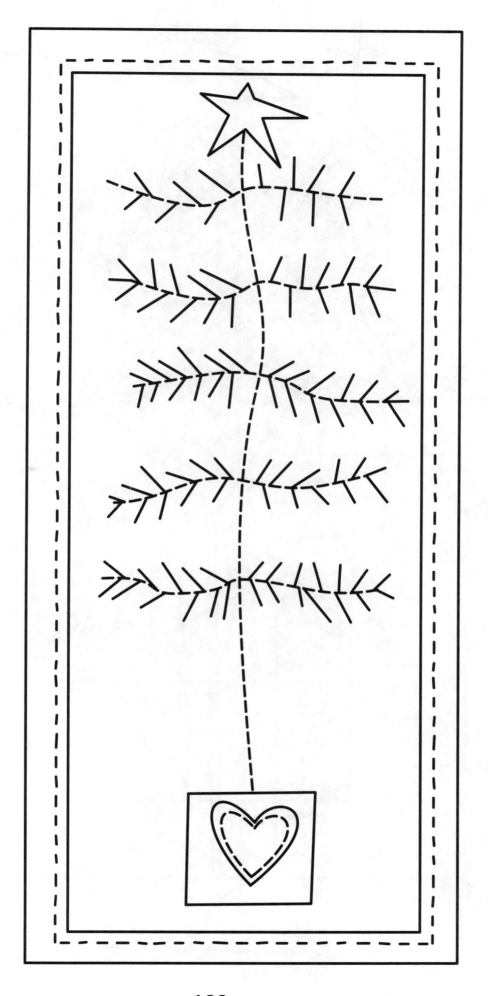

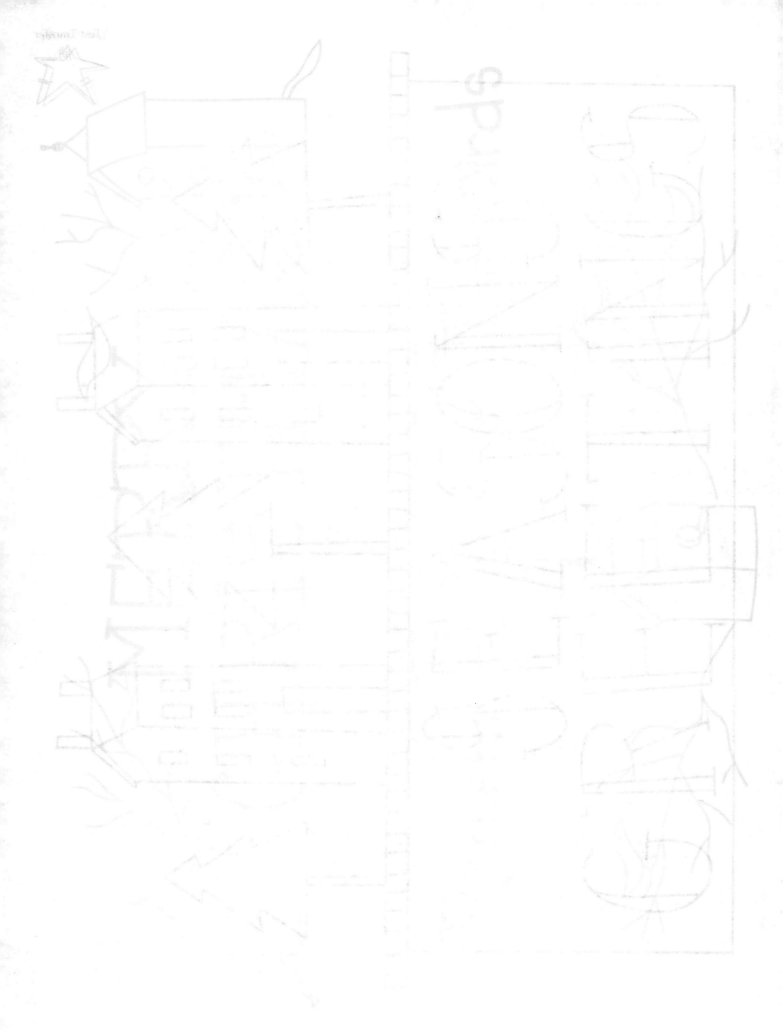

Test Transfer

MERRY CHRISTMAS

Remember The best of Birds

138

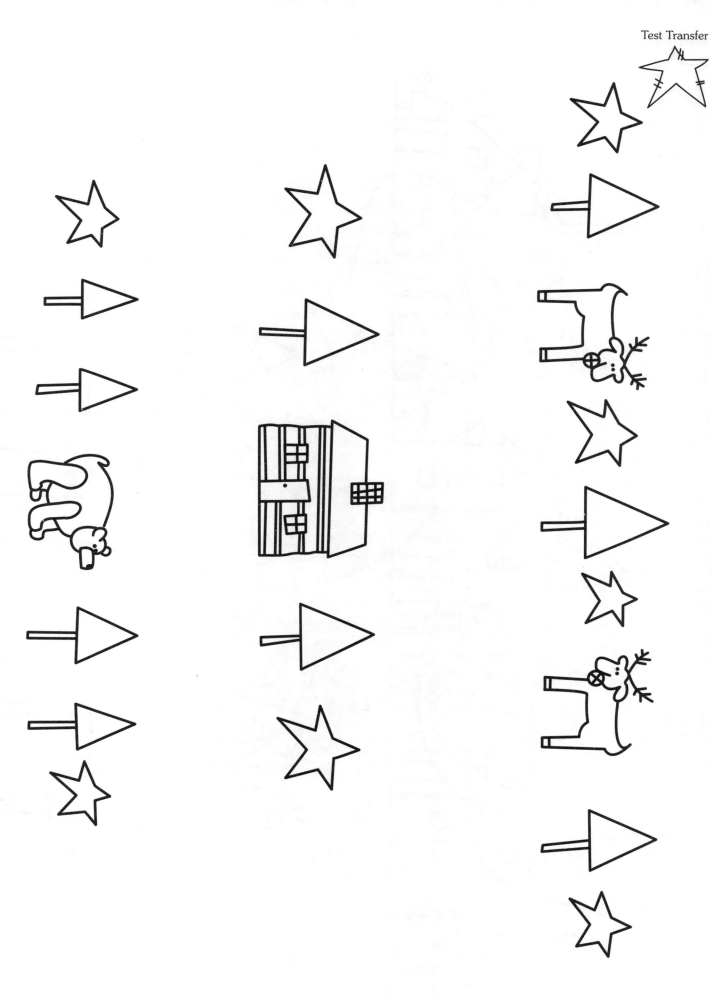

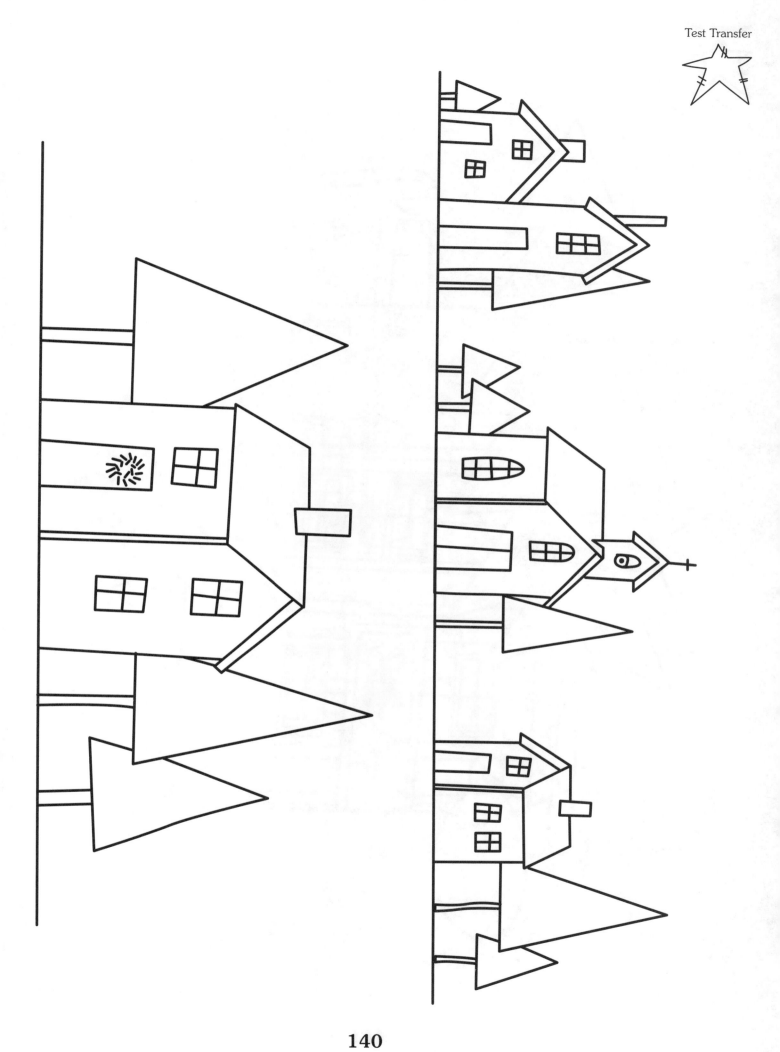

Test Transfer

140

141

Test Transfer

A✻NORTHWOOD✻CHRISTMAS

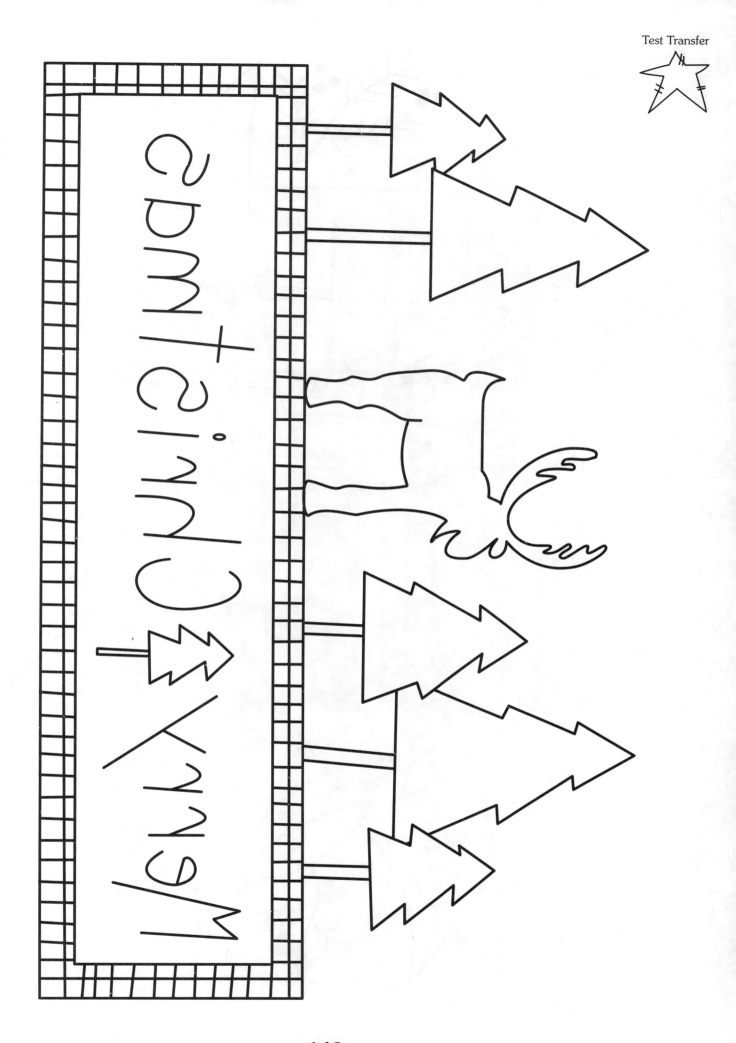

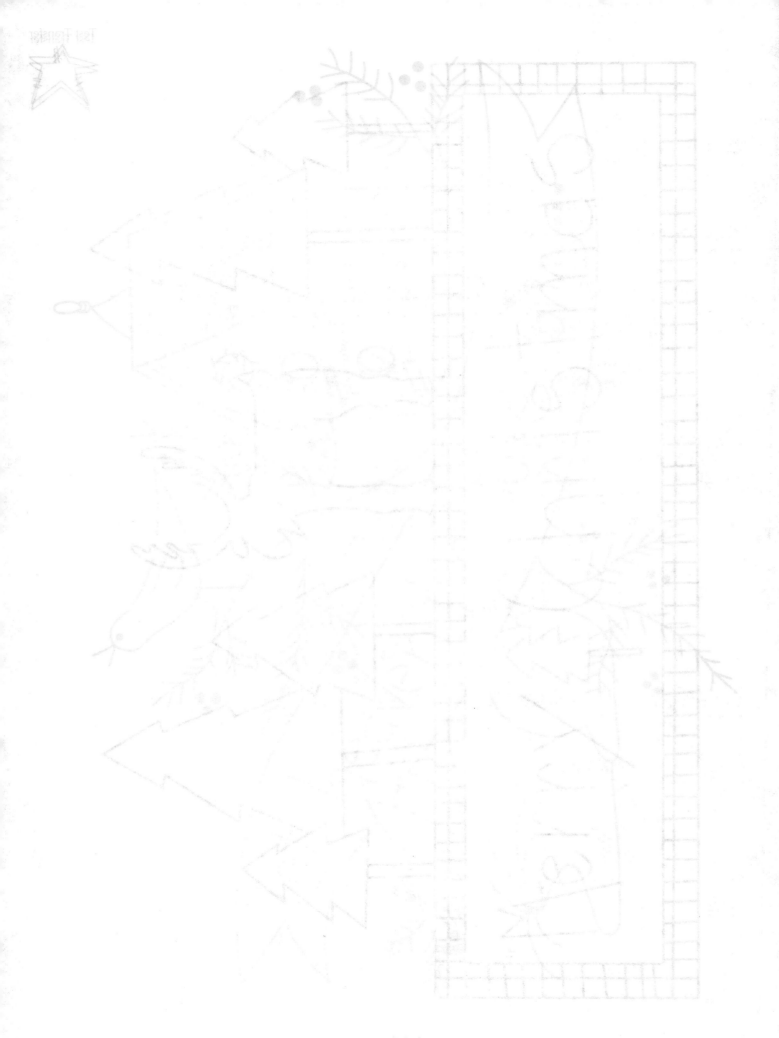

Greetings Season's ...House Your To House Our From

148

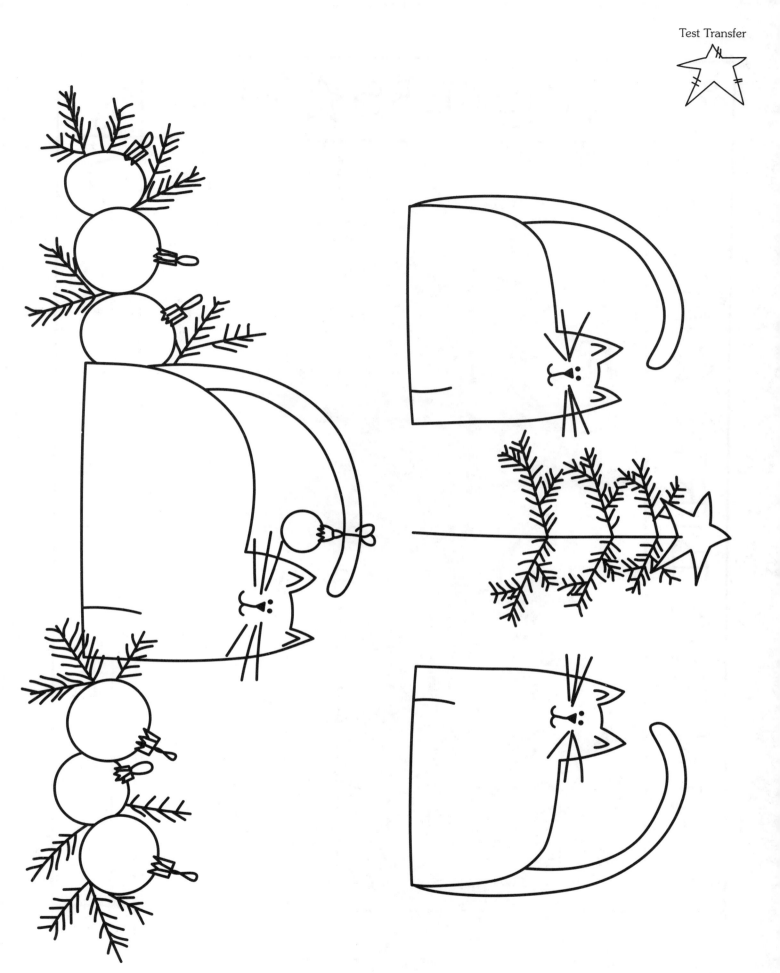

151

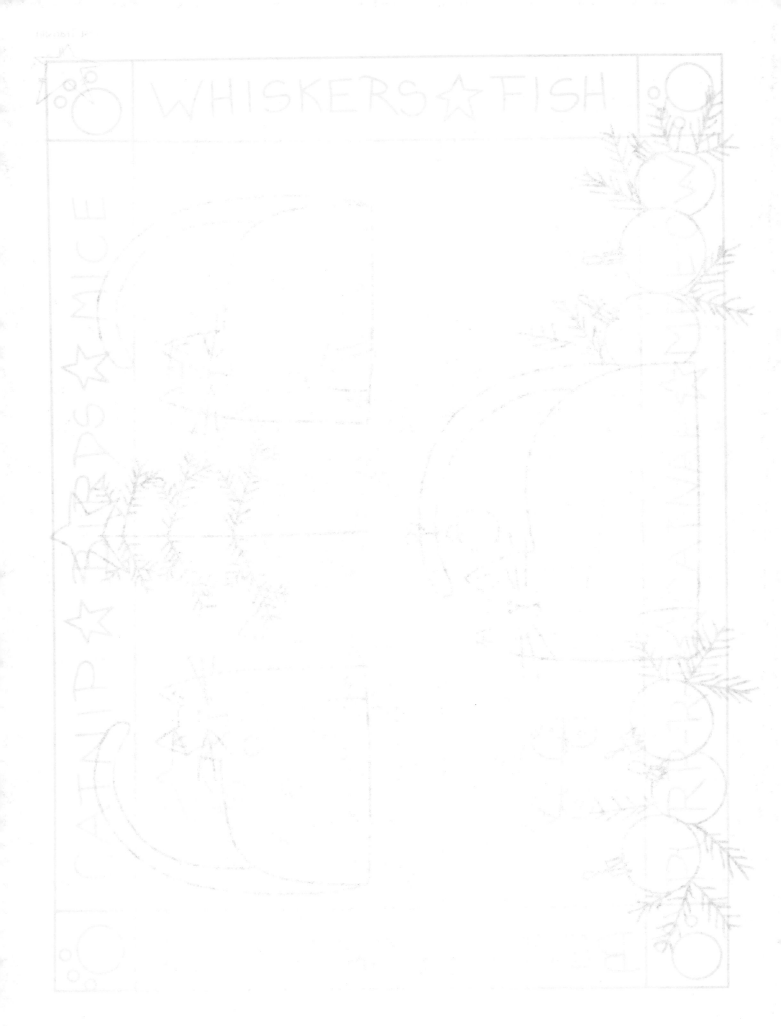

152

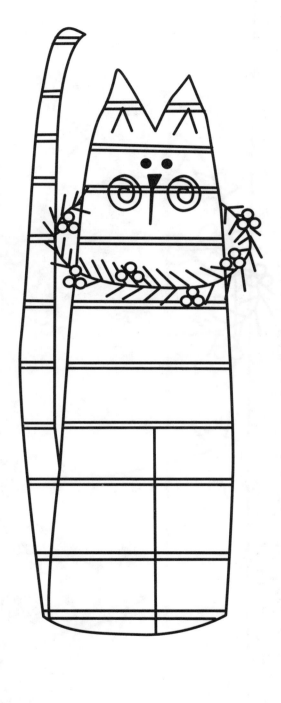

Merry Christmas

The Twas The Night Before Christmas...

155

156

157

158

Makin' a list, checkin' it twice...

Gonna find out who's

naughty and nice!

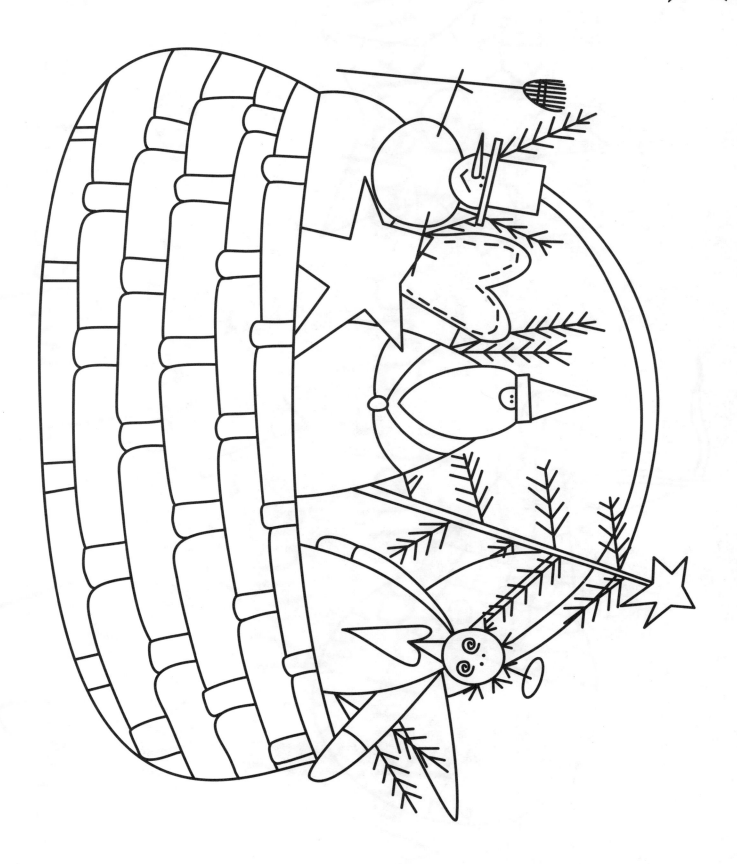

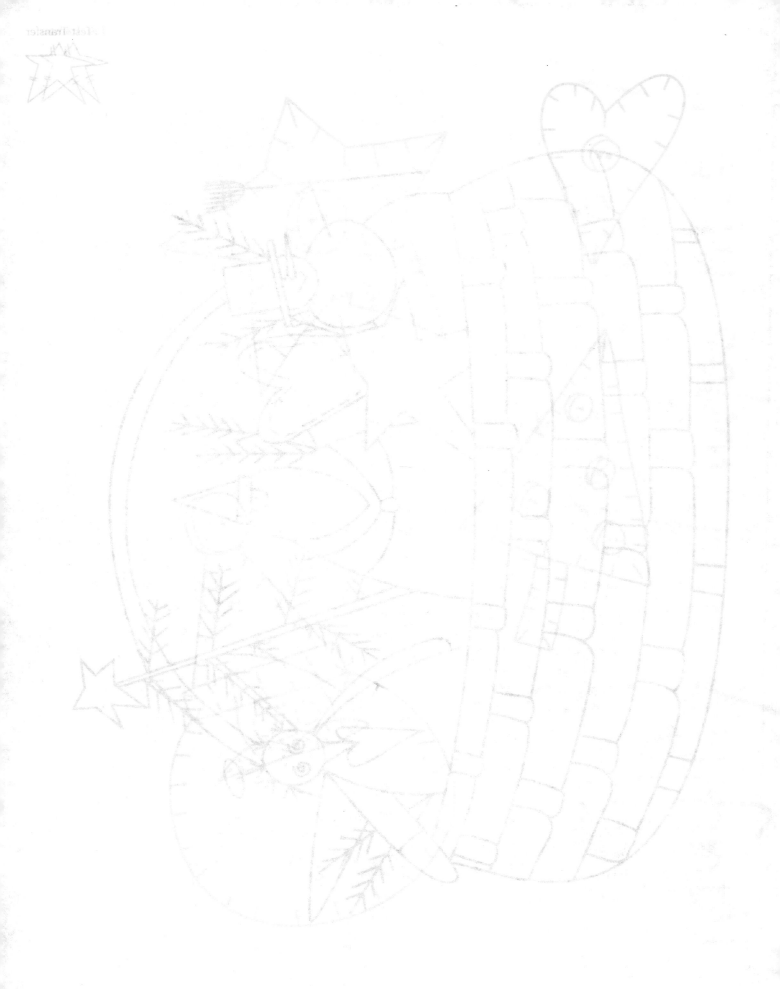

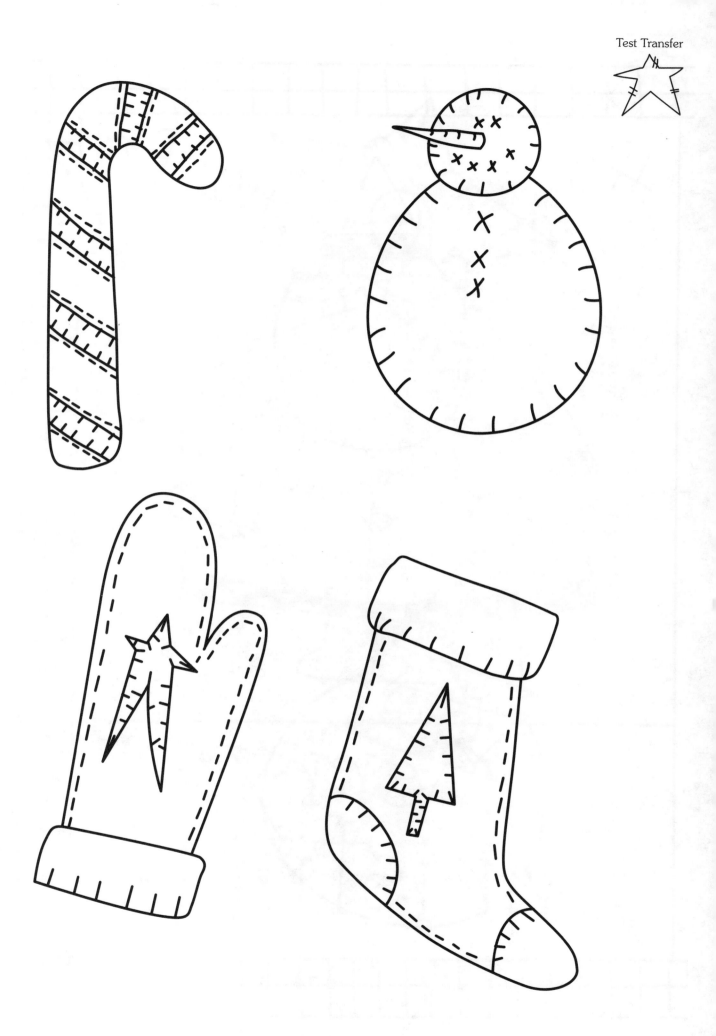